Never, EVER, Quit!

Jane Hoeppner
with Terry Hutchens

Blue River Press
Indianapolis

Cover designed by Phil Velikan
Proofread by H. Lowhorn
Packaged by Wish Publishing

Printed in the United States of America
10 9 8 7 6 5 4 3 2 1

Distributed in the United States by
Cardinal Publishers Group
www.cardinalpub.com

Song Title: VOICE OF TRUTH
Writer Credits: MARK HALL / STEVEN CURTIS CHAPMAN
Copyright: © 2003 Sparrow Song (BMI) Club Zoo Music (BMI) SWECS Music (BMI) My Refuge Music (BMI) Peach Hill Songs (BMI) (adm. by EMI CMG Publishing). All rights reserved. Used by permission.

Song Title: HOLD FAST
Writer Credits: Bart Millard/Nathan Cochran/Barry Graul/Mike Scheuchzer/Robby Shaffer
Copyright: © 2006 Simpleville Music & Wet as a Fish Music (ASCAP). All rights adim. by Simpleville Music, Inc. All rights reserved. Used by permission.

Song Title: BRING THE RAIN
Writer Credits: Bart Millard/Nathan Cochran/Barry Graul/Mike Scheuchzer/Robby Shaffer
Copyright: © 2006 Simpleville Music & Wet as a Fish Music (ASCAP). All rights adim. by Simpleville Music, Inc. All rights reserved. Used by permission.

Both authors would like to dedicate this book to loved ones.

"This book is lovingly dedicated to Amy, Allison and Drew who have shared my tears and laughter and loss. I count each of you as my 'for such a time as this' blessings. To my sons-in-law Steve and Drew, you have made it easy for me to love you as my own. And to my parents, Paul and Dorothy Madinger, who have remained steadfast in their prayers and unwavering in their love. Last of all, I dedicate these pages to Terry's 'wills to live' — Tucker, Spencer, Tate and Quinny. Pa would be so proud!"
— Jane Hoeppner

"Working with Jane on this project has served as a reminder of the strong women of faith who have been such an important part of the fabric of my life. Three in particular come quickly to mind. First, my mother, Dena Hutchens, who has done so well surviving and thriving amidst adversity since the passing of my father in June of 2000. Secondly, my mother-in-law, Jean Hamme, who taught me a great deal about selflessness as she cared for my father-in-law who became wheelchair bound late in life. Jean went to be with our Lord in 2003, but her spirit is strong in our family. Finally, my wife Susan, who is the strongest woman I have ever had the privilege to know. Having raised three boys, myself included, she has earned her place in heaven."
— Terry Hutchens

Table of Contents

Preface

The first time Jane Hoeppner and I met to discuss doing this book was at the Barnes and Noble in Greenwood, Ind., in late May of 2009. As we sat at a rickety table set up for coffee shop patrons outside the store, we prayed for God to show us the way. We met that day believing that we wanted to write a book together but at the same time arrived with open minds. If this project was of Him, we felt we would know it right away. If it didn't feel right, we would walk away and that would be OK, too.

We talked that day about the kinds of things we thought His people would want to read. We talked about the way the book could be presented and the kind of encouragement such an undertaking could ultimately provide. We talked about how we thought the book had a chance to make a difference and how the story and message was one that needed to be shared.

An hour later we were confident that the affirmation we were feeling from each other was a sign that this was a book that He wanted us to do. We never really considered any other title than *Never, EVER, Quit*. It seemed perfect and there was no reason to mess with perfection.

Through the process of writing the book, the confidence that we felt that first day never wavered. When we think of acknowledgements for a book such as this one, it's overwhelming clear that all of the glory goes to our God and Savior who has been with us every step of the way. He gets the glory. We were just lucky enough to be the people he chose as his earthen vessels to share the message.

Whenever we struggled at any point in this journey, God was quick to provide. When we asked three friends to review the book for the back cover, Joani Crean, Tammy Walker and Brenda Roethlisberger were quick to agree to help us. When we needed help with compiling pictures and scripture verses for the reference section at the end of the book, Jane's three children, Amy, Allison and Drew, all sprang into action. We can't thank them enough, not only for their 11th hour contributions but also for adding details to different events that were written about in these pages.

When we weren't sure who was going to handle the photography for the cover of the book, April Knox was clearly an answer to prayer. Jane talks in this book about different people who came along at different times who were like hugs from God. April was one of those people. As a photographer, she was as professional as can be and worked with Jane to make the final selection just right. The fact that she was a woman of faith was abundantly clear from the first time we met her. She had been hand-picked by God to come to our aid. There's no question about that. At the end of the book, there is an 'About the Photographer' page where you can learn more about April and hopefully take advantage of her photography services in the future.

Of course, there are others we would like to thank as well. Tom Doherty with Cardinal Publishers Group believed in the project and provided us the avenue with which we needed to get it published. This is the third book I've written with Tom, and he has always been extremely easy to work with. Holly Kondras handled the layout, pagination and photos and also made the process less stressful at the end. *The Indianapolis Star* allowed me to write the book and to complete it during college football season which was very much appreciated.

Both Jane and I would like to thank our respective families for their support as we completed this project. You don't truly understand and appreciate the time commitment until you've written a book like this. But there is time away from family, and it would be an insurmountable task without the support of loved ones. I'd like to thank my wife Susan for allowing me to pursue another dream of writing a book, and my boys Bryan and Kevin for their support of this venture as well.

When I wrote the book '*Hep Remembered*' in 2007, I ended the acknowledgements by thanking Hep himself for the inspiration he provided me during the writing process. He had passed away a few months earlier, but his spirit was alive in that book. "Have a plan. Work the plan. Plan for the unexpected," was one of Hep's favorite sayings that constantly echoed through my mind when I was engaged in that project and in this one.

With *Never, EVER, Quit* Hep inspired me in a different way. Early in the summer of 2009 I was finding it difficult to motivate myself to sit down and write some of the early chapters after long interview sessions I had conducted with Jane. One day, I was sitting at the computer with writer's block, and I glanced at a copy of *Hep Remembered* on the shelf near my work area. In the cover photo, Hep is pointing straight ahead. It was a photo that the university had used on its football schedule poster one year with the slogan, 'Hep Wants You.' When I looked at the book cover, I felt as if Hep was pointing at me. Yes, he wanted me, but what he really wanted was for me to get busy.

And I did. In fact, I picked up two copies of the book and put one on each side of the keyboard to use as motivation. Whenever my mind would wander, Hep and I would make eye contact, and I'd get right back to work. So, thanks, Hep, for your continued inspiration and motivation.

I hope you enjoy reading the book as much as we enjoyed writing it. Our belief is that if something in these pages can make a difference in a single life than this project will have been a tremendous success.

— Terry Hutchens

Prologue

Never, EVER, Quit.

Used together, spoken slowly, with an emphasis on 'Ever', those are three powerful words. Sometimes their message is easier said than done. But there is something compelling about those words.

My late husband, Terry Hoeppner, will forever be remembered for the way he lived his "Don't Quit" mantra. It was a part of his very being. It was the directive he had for his players at Indiana University, Miami University, Franklin College and other stops along the way. He also imparted it to our children and it influenced how they approached their daily lives.

Most importantly, it was right there in the heart of his eighteen month battle with brain cancer that ultimately took his life on June 19, 2007. But it's also the message he passed on to me to remind others to never give up the fight. It's a message that God has reinforced in my soul. As my husband said in so many speeches over the years, it's always too soon to quit. I believed it when I first heard him say that, and I believe it even more now.

The first time I remember Terry using the "Don't Quit" poem was in 1980 while speaking at an athletic awards dinner in Ft. Wayne, Ind. At the time he was coaching at East Noble High School in Kendallville, Ind. Terry and I always shared a love for books, but unlike me, he preferred having several going at the same time. One would usually be a mystery — à la W.E.B. Griffin or Clive Cussler — the other a biography or book on leadership. He was always interested in knowing how people had attained a level of excellence in their chosen field. He was intrigued with the fact that regardless of the profession, these achievers shared a commonality. Each had learned to persevere. And so it's not surprising that never quitting would be the hallmark of our life together. In the face of adversity or challenge, we never threw in the towel. Our belief was simple — if you don't quit, you have a chance.

In 1986 we had a difficult decision to make in terms of Terry's coaching future. We had returned to Franklin College in 1980 when Terry became the defensive coordinator for his mentor and college coach, Red Faught. He was involved in all the decision-making within the program and seemed to be the heir-apparent whenever Coach Faught decided to retire.

But in '86, a position opened at Miami University, a Division I school in Oxford, Ohio. Sports buffs would know that it is called the Cradle of Coaches. Often times in the coaching business a single event will trigger a domino effect on job openings. This was the case when Dave McClain, the coach at Wisconsin, died unexpectedly.

As a result of that, an opportunity presented itself

for us to go to Miami. They were interested in Terry, but I wasn't sure if it was the right time for a change. Would the kids adjust? Could I find a teaching job? I had some reservations and lots of questions. Many prayers were sent up asking for divine intervention. That's when we met Victor.

I've told this story many times in speaking engagements over the last two years because it is such a remarkable and humorous example of a life-lesson learned. This lesson came in the form of a bird of all things!

I was teaching a summer enrichment class at the college. Dismissal was at noon and Terry would meet me to go home for lunch together. As I was waiting outside the administration building, I couldn't help hearing the loud squawking of a bird close to the spot where I was standing. I looked down at the grass and immediately saw the reason for the very upset mother bird. Her baby had fallen from the nest and found itself in a precarious place.

After sizing up the tree and deciding there was no way Terry (not me, of course!) could climb it and return the bird its nest, I went to Plan B. My husband had arrived by this time and watched as I went inside to find some kind of container. We were soon on our way home with our rescued "baby" safely inside a cardboard envelope box. The kids were thrilled, but we knew nothing about birds.

Amy suggested calling her biology teacher. We did, but he was less than optimistic, pointing out birds that size can't survive without their mothers. Our next thought was a woman in town called the Bird Lady. Surely someone with a nickname like that would be helpful. She wasn't a lot more encouraging, but said we should treat it the way we would an infant. It should be fed baby cereal every three to four hours using an eye dropper. The Bird Lady also told us that if the baby cereal feeding was successful, we could try chopping up worms for dessert!

Amy, Allison and Drew were in charge of meal-time with one person holding the bird (wrapped in a washcloth) and the other operating the eye dropper. By now the bird had been christened Victor (no one knows why), and he began to know the routine. When the eye dropper appeared overhead, he knew something good was about to happen.

During one of his feedings, when Drew had the dropper detail, Victor got excited, jumped up and the dropper literally dropped. It dropped down into his throat! We had lots of tears and "Oh, no, we've killed the bird," But the only telltale sign of the close call was Victor's permanently hoarse chirp. And so this bird with dried cereal on its neck and a uniquely raspy voice became part of our family.

He was definitely a 'people' bird and would follow us everywhere. After much prompting, Victor began to fly from low branches to the ground. However, we were never able to teach him how to peck for worms and any food that he got came from the eye dropper. After several weeks and many funny Victor stories, he flew off and didn't return. We were happy because of his independence, but sad because he had not learned how to feed himself.

It was at this same time that we were making plans to head to Miami University and tackling some feelings of uncertainty that always come with the unknown.

At about 6 o'clock one Saturday morning Terry and I were awakened by a sound that we both knew. Sitting up in bed, we looked at each other and said, "Victor!" As we heard that hoarse chirping, we jumped out of bed and ran to the window. There, sitting on the fence with a little dried cereal still on its neck, was our bird.

But it was now obvious that Victor was in fact Victoria. She had her handsome husband with her and they were quite a sight to see. As we stood there in amazement at our friend's return, she flew down to the ground right below the window where we were standing.

She then proceeded to pull out the biggest worm you've ever seen. It was a God moment for us. We knew that if He watched over a robin and even allowed us to witness that care in such a personal way, we would be looked after as well. Everything was going to be fine. So, on to Oxford we went — and, yes, there was a job waiting for me and each of our children would receive Miami degrees.

After arriving at Miami, the famous "Don't Quit" poem became part of Terry's message. He had opportunities for speaking engagements, and it became an expected part of his delivery. I can hear him saying those words still.

When things go wrong as they sometimes will,
And the road you're trudging seems all up hill,
When the funds are low and the debts are high,
When you want to smile, but you have to sigh,
When care is pressing you down a bit,
Rest if you must, but don't you quit.

For life is strange with its twist and turns,
As every one of us sometimes learns,
But many a coward turns about,
When he might have won had he stuck it out;
But he learns too late when the night comes down,
How close he was to the golden crown.

Victory is defeat turned inside out,
The silver tint of the clouds of doubt,

You will never know how near you are,
It may be close when it seems afar,
So stick to the fight when you are hardest hit,
It's when things seem worst that you must not quit.
— Anonymous

It was while we were in Oxford in the 1990s that we really had some life experiences to put some meat around those bones.

We began to understand how powerful the bond of marriage is and the reward of hanging in there during difficult times. As friends and lovers we found contentment in each other and so enjoyed the pleasure of each other's company. Our commitment to one another was a deep and lasting one, but it didn't happen overnight. There is something to be said about going shoulder to shoulder toward the same goal. We shared dreams and looked forward to the future. The anticipation of something can be exciting as well as motivating. If we lose our forward-thinking, we lose hope. Who can last long without hope?

My husband spent more years as an assistant than he did as a head coach. To be able to maintain his level of enthusiasm and energy spoke to the kind of person he was. Terry was a company man. He didn't have much use for networking and would say, "Take care of the job that you have right now, and the next one will take care of itself." I think there are valuable lessons to be learned there, too. Whatever the task, do it to the best of your ability and everything else will work out. It sounds simple, but it does require some faith.

Terry had plans for us to write a book together when he retired and when we would have the time to commit to such an undertaking. The last thing I ever envisioned was doing a book by myself.

As a coach's wife, I sat through many dinners at

Terry's side and listened to more speeches than I can recall. Never did I picture myself up there providing the message. I was content to be what I call a professional listener. But I am finding that desires can and do change. I feel as if God has given me a voice and has provided opportunities for me to use it. He has helped me overcome the doubt and fear that comes with standing in front of a group and telling my story.

God has a plan and a purpose for each of us. Where I am today and how I got here are not the way I would have scripted it. Terry and I were so intertwined as one, that it was impossible to grasp what life would be with that part of me missing. But God has helped me know that He understands my loss and all that comes with it. He has continued to provide the peace and strength that I so desperately need to persevere and finish strong.

This book is my answer to God's prompting and gentle nudging. As I set out with my friend Terry Hutchens to write it, my prayer is that hearts will be open to the encouragement and hope it offers.

I pray that you will know the profound love that our Heavenly Father has for each of his children and feel His arms hugging you tightly. May these pages inspire you to seek Him with more purpose and claim those three simple words as your own.

Never, EVER, Quit.

Part One

1

My Best Friend

The first time I laid eyes on Terry Hoeppner was in French class when we were freshmen at Franklin College in Franklin, Ind. The students were seated in alphabetical order which meant Hoeppner was in the row in front of Madinger. I still have to smile when I think about my long-legged, athletic-looking classmate doing battle with the wooden desk that was not quite big enough for his tall frame. He never did find a comfortable position, but it didn't seem to keep him from occasionally nodding off. In his defense he had completed three years of high school French and had no problem maintaining a B average! At some point he asked me out, but I turned him down because I was dating someone else. What was I thinking?

The grant-in-aid for my tuition required me to work a certain number of hours per week. My first placement was as a server at the dining room at Elsey Hall, the women's dormitory. At that time the women and men ate separately and there was an expectation of proper table decorum. All the ladies gathered in the lobby at 6 p.m. and were dismissed to the dining room when the chimes rang. The meal was served family-style with an upperclassman at each table acting as the hostess. After dessert the group was dismissed altogether. It seems strange to think of how different it was then. Times were changing, though, and that would be the last year for the women-only dining hall.

In second semester I began working in the football office for Red Faught. When I say office, I really mean room. It was a space big enough for Coach Faught's desk, and my small desk was in a corner facing the wall. There were several chairs for guests and a file cabinet. The best part about the office was the picture that hung on the wall behind Coach's desk. It was a large black and white action picture of the New York Giants and the St. Louis Cardinals. It proved to be a conversation piece for anyone who came into the office and it continued to occupy a place of honor even when Coach moved to a new facility. That picture now hangs in my study, a gift to Terry from Coach Faught when he got the IU job.

At the beginning of our sophomore year, Terry and I went out on our first date to a Phi Delt house dance. I was still working as the football secretary which enabled us to run into each other regularly. There was just something about him. I can remember Coach Faught telling me once that Terry was wise beyond his years. We valued Coach's opinion, and I never forgot his insightful description.

Our history together had begun. I fell in love with a small town boy, and he loved his city girl. Indianapolis, not New York! We talked about the future and wondered what it held. I found out how passionate he was about football, and he was fascinated that I had come from a musical household.

As that school year ended, we each went home to our summer jobs and had to be content with phone calls and letters. I was hired at Goodman Jewelers in a local mall and learned a little about working in retail. Terry's birthday was in August, and I decided to surprise him with a handmade sweater vest. The only problem was I didn't know how to knit. My dilemma was solved when I found out that one of my co-workers was an expert knitter. She had been born in Switzerland and learned to crochet and knit at an early age. Everyday she would accompany me to lunch so she could help me with my stitches, which I seemed to have a habit of dropping. By the time August 19th rolled around, only half of the vest was finished. So I put it into half of a box with half of a bow and half of a card. He didn't get the whole sweater until Christmas!

That fall we were back into the school routine with football season and classes. We shared an exciting Homecoming in October when Terry ran back an interception for a touchdown, and I was crowned Homecoming Queen. It was a perfect day. When I look at the picture of us taken after the game, I am struck at how young we look. We had no inkling of the road that lay ahead.

After Christmas of our junior year Terry and I found out that we were expecting. This was not the idyllic beginning to married life that I had envisioned. We talked to our parents and decided on a March wedding date. Our families were supportive of our marriage plans and helped us through this tumultuous time. We couldn't have done it without their wisdom and love.

Amy was born in September, a beauty with lots of energy. As the first grandchild on both sides of the family, she held a special place in everyone's heart and was the object of much attention. I became a full-time mom and, surprisingly, didn't miss school. Terry played football that fall and graduated in May. We understood the odds were against us making it as a family, but Terry and I were determined that we would not be a statistic.

We left Franklin to begin the coaching life at Eastbrook High School in Upland, Ind. Our first house was a rental on what we called Sewer Street because the only traffic we saw was trucks going to the treatment plant. Terry was teaching eighth grade science and physical education. He was an assistant for the high school team and also coached junior high basketball. Amy was the mascot for the team and wore her little E sweater and red skirt at the games.

The next year Terry was promoted to head football coach, and we moved to Van Buren, the other feeder town for Eastbrook. It was also at this time that we found out that we were expecting again. On the morning of March 5th 1971, I knew that it would be the day our family would welcome the new addition. Terry went to school as usual, but I called him at lunchtime and said he needed to come home. We still had one more item of business before this baby was born — choosing the name! We vacillated between Allison and Aubrey for our girl. Jeffrey was our choice for a boy.

We headed to Marion General Hospital at around 5 p.m., but by the time we arrived the contractions had slowed down. I made Terry drive around town until they picked up again. We checked in at 6:30, and Allison Lynn was born at 8:15 p.m. There is something awe-inspiring about seeing your brand new baby. She was gorgeous with beautiful eyes, and I couldn't wait to get her home.

There were strict rules regarding who could visit the maternity floor. Only immediate family members were allowed and then no more than two at a time. Knowing the rule, but anxious to see the new baby, two of our friends came up the back way to my room for a clandestine visit. They got to briefly see Allison before they were unceremoniously escorted out. How times have changed!

We eventually left Eastbrook when Terry had a try-out with the Green Bay Packers. He had played semi-pro ball with the Indianapolis Caps and that led to the offer from the Packers. He was the last one cut which is of little consolation when he had given so much effort and heart. My girls and I had stayed with Terry's family in Woodburn while he was away. We also had a chance to visit my parents who had moved to Birmingham, Ala., where my dad had become the chaplain at the VA hospital there.

With our family back together, we looked at what the next step would be. That would be one of the hardest years of our married life. He briefly sold insurance until he realized he was not a salesman. Next he taught high school chemistry, and that was even worse. After Christmas we moved to Birmingham where he got a job teaching PE and coaching spring football.

Our apartment was five minutes from my parents which was a God-send. Terry was still chasing the dream of playing ball and signed on with the Detroit Wheels of the World Football League. That meant moving back north to Ypsilanti, Mich. We would be there for that season and then back to Birmingham for the spring semester of teaching.

If you're having trouble following this, I understand. I lived it, and it's still confusing! The next year he played for the Charlotte Hornets and that's where we were living when the WFL folded. On a happier note, it's also where our son Drew was born in 1976. Our family was completed with this chubby, easy-going baby boy.

The five of us would go south from Charlotte to Mullins, South Carolina. Terry was hired as athletic director and head football coach at Mullins High School. His interview took place at the cotton ginnery owned by the school board president. The board members peppered Terry with questions while perched on their rickety stools and old chairs.

It wasn't until after we arrived in town that we found out about the lawsuit against the school district. Apparently the previous football and basketball staffs had been fired, but were not given due process. They in turn sued the school district. So within a month of being on the job, Terry found himself in Columbia, S.C., testifying on behalf of the Mullins School District. The suit was settled out of court with part of the agreement being the reassignment of the fired coaches. This task was the responsibility of my husband, the new athletic director. It was a rather daunting beginning for what would be a character-building time for both of us.

There were still more challenges that awaited us, including the high school burning down the first week of school. Integration had recently come to this small southern town, and there were strong opinions held by many. Our team was called the Auctioneers because Mullins was referred to as the Tobacco Capital of the World. There were huge warehouses in town where the auctioneers would sell the tobacco to the highest bidder. Many of our players worked during the harvesting of the crop and practice times might be changed according to how many were "cropping."

Terry was not only the A.D. and coach, but he was also in charge of preparing the field for games. My kids still remember playing on the cinder track while their dad and I got the string straight before laying down that line of chalk. We replaced burned out light bulbs and made sure the restrooms had toilet paper. It was probably during this time that Terry came up with his phrase, "No job is too small." The obstacles that we had to overcome did not compare to the value of the people who became part of our lives. He put together a winning program, and we came away with life-long friends. As was the case at all of our coaching stops, the relationships formed would be the most treasured part.

There are many memories of special people who were in our lives for a reason. On our first Mother's Day in Mullins we had an unexpected visit from two of our players, Nathan and Mark Gerald. They had a gift for me — a beautiful silver necklace! I was surprised and proud of how thoughtful these two young men had been. Mark would eventually become the principal of Mullins High School. Our quarterback and wide receiver were identical twins, Lynn and Glenn Martin. Their mom, Eva, became my friend and confidante while dad, Jerry, was the unofficial videotaper of all our games. We stayed close after leaving Mullins and enjoyed seeing the twins every few years when they would visit. The twins would eventually bring their own sons, and it was wonderful to see what great fathers they had each become.

Our time in Mullins ended on an exciting note for me. Early in the spring of that year there were auditions being held for a community theatre production of *The Music Man*. I was in the church choir and also directed the children's Angel Choir at Macedonia Methodist. Terry asked if I was interested in trying out and knowing how much time would be involved I responded no. Our kids were ten, eight and three and I couldn't see how this was remotely possible. Unknown to me, he got a copy of the audition script and brought it home. He was insistent that I at least give it a try and assured me that he would take care of the children.

And so a nervous thirty-two-year-old mom sat through the beautiful renderings of much younger women, becoming more positive with each one that I had no shot at getting the part of Marian the Librarian. But I **DID** get the part and Terry found out there was more to keeping the home fires burning than he ever imagined!

It was during these weeks of preparation for the musical that we were also getting ready to move back to Indiana. To say that it was a busy time is an understatement. The show times were set for Friday through Sunday, June 7th, 8th and 9th. On the Monday after the last performance, we would be heading north to Kendallville, Ind. in our fully loaded U-Haul. Our parents had come as well to be a part of our last event in South Carolina. *The Music Man* was a success and a thrilling experience for me. Amy and Allison were also on stage as members of the town's band, so it really was a family affair. My best friend was also my biggest fan, and it was fun to have him in the audience cheering for me rather than the other way around.

After a year in Kendallville at East Noble High School, we would begin our journey into college coaching. At Coach Faught's request, we returned to Franklin and Terry became his defensive coordinator. He also taught several classes which is usually part of the job description for coaches at small colleges. Our children settled into their schools, and we enjoyed being in a community that was very familiar to us.

It wasn't long before I decided that this would be the perfect time for me to finish my degree. My major had been physical education, but I now realized that elementary education was where I needed to be. As I studied my transcript, I saw that on my last semester's grades an incomplete for a class had been changed to an F. This happens if you don't complete the course work, and I obviously had not. Because of the impact of that failing grade, my GPA was not where I wanted it to be.

After much thought, I made the choice to retake the class. It required deliberation on my part because the class was team sports and I was now 36 years old. It would mean actually doing the activities, not just reading about them. I still recall sitting in the car with Terry outside the gym dressed in my new warm-up. I felt like a kindergartener on the first day of school, and my heart was pounding when I finally made my way inside. Somehow I made it through all of the dive rolls in the volleyball section and ended up with an A to replace the F!

Our tenure at Franklin would last for six years. I graduated from college the same year Amy graduated from high school. When we left for Miami University in Oxford, Ohio, Amy had already been accepted at Franklin. She would complete her first two years there.

For Allison the transition was difficult. She was beginning her sophomore year in high school and had made the cheerleading squad before we moved. Now she was in a situation where those positions had already been filled and she was looking at how she would fit into this new school setting. She tried out and made the tennis team, and it provided friendships that helped pave the way. Drew was starting fifth grade and also had to find his place among strange faces and new teachers. Being a part of the football staff also gave them a chance to be with other children who shared their dilemma.

My teaching career began at Kramer Elementary, and I would spend 15 years in third grade! I was a language arts curriculum coordinator for two years after I left the classroom. The colleagues that I taught with became close friends and made my school days richer. I would tell my students on a regular basis, "There's no place I would rather be than right here with you!"

The timing of my teaching career was perfect. I was

old enough to have more insights and young enough to enjoy the energy level of 8 year olds. Amy, Allison and Drew all received Miami degrees. Being on campus where your dad is a coach has its advantages as well as its drawbacks. Terry and I hoped they had the college experience even though they were only five minutes from home!

Because our family was in Oxford for 19 years, we went through many phases of life. There were graduations and weddings, and we even became grandparents. Amy had married her college sweetheart, Steve, and they proceeded to give us the incredible gift of Tucker. We had thought all the talk about the virtues of being a grandparent was overrated. That line of thinking went right out the window the minute we saw Tucker. Terry had an 'out of body' experience and Aunt Allison and Uncle Drew were just as smitten as we were. Our affection knew no bounds!

Spencer followed his brother two years later and once again we were in love. He was loaded with his Pa's (Terry) persistence and competitiveness, but had a soft spot for Mim (me). Our blessings would continue as Allison and her husband, Drew, gifted us with Tate. He is so similar in nature and build to his Pa. Tate's little brother, Quinn, came along three years later. My mother was in the room and witnessed his birth. That was a first for her at the age of 82.

Through these experiences my best friend and I began to have a new appreciation for each other. I've heard some people talk about their children being gone and how they feel like life is over. They have nothing in common with their spouse and have found that they have grown apart. Maybe it was because we didn't have all of the alone time at the beginning of our marriage, but we more than made up for it at the end.

Terry deeply appreciated how I had been there for

our kids when his job kept him busy. He now looked for ways that he could honor that commitment. One means that he employed was to make sure I was beside him on the team bus or plane. There are some coaches that follow this practice, while for others this situation would not be tenable. However, he insisted on it and never made me feel as though I was a distraction. On the contrary, we had many heart-to-heart talks on the way home after games and looked forward to the companionship we shared. We enjoyed traveling together even on those road trips with the team. I took along reading or work to occupy me, while he was busy with meetings and attending to any last minute game preparation. We found such strength in how we operated as a couple. We made each other better.

Our tradition of greeting each other on the field after games was a long-standing one. It was, of course, more enjoyable after a win, but nonetheless happened after every game. Terry was well-known for his feelings about losing, and he never lost his competitive edge. After a loss my kids and I knew it was better not to ask about certain plays or calls until he had eaten and had a chance to sit in his recliner. He put so much time and effort into his craft that he took each defeat personally.

But being his grandson afforded Spencer influence that not everyone had. After a particularly stinging defeat, Terry had been sitting sullenly in his chair for quite a while. Three year old Spence had patiently waited and finally reached his limit. Walking up to the recliner, he tugged Terry's sleeve and said, "Pa, the game is over!" He looked down at those big blue eyes and saw the unconditional love in them. Spencer didn't care if his team won or lost, he just wanted his Pa.

When we took the IU job, people were surprised that we would leave our children. They really are fully-grown, highly-functioning adults, but the closeness of our family had become common knowledge.

Our welcome to Indiana University in December of 2004 was overwhelming. The city of Bloomington and the state of Indiana fell in love with Coach Hep, and he basked in the glow of that affection. He returned the love and his sincerity and depth of gratitude were never in doubt.

The spring and summer of 2005 were a whirlwind of speaking engagements and all that goes along with changing a culture in a few short months. He was laying the foundation that was necessary for a strong and lasting program. Terry got to reap the rewards of doing things the right way. He got his dream job, and I got to share it with him.

Two football traditions that Terry started at Indiana were the Rock and the Walk. Memorial Stadium is built on and made of the limestone for which our area of the state is so well known. It seemed only natural that limestone should be part of our football persona. And so from the pile of leftover boulders from the construction of Memorial Stadium, one 'manly' one was chosen. The three-ton rock was secured on a base and placed by the end zone for players and coaches and fans to touch. It became an incredible connection for everyone.

As for the Walk, two hours before kickoff the Hoosiers get off the buses on Woodlawn and make their way across 17th Street to Assembly Hall and then head into the stadium. Fans line both sides of the walk and greet the players and extend their well wishes. When they reach the stairs next to Assembly Hall, the IU Marching Hundred is there to salute them in music. Unless you've experienced it, you can't describe the energy and excitement that the players and fans enjoy. It's great!

It's amazing how those two things lend themselves to spiritual analogies. People would ask if we did it on purpose. No, we didn't. But looking back, I'm sure someone who could see the whole picture understood the parallels. We were about to truly walk the walk and know exactly how it feels to lean on the Solid Rock.

2

Signs of Trouble
The First Surgery

Thanksgiving was always one of my husband's favorite times of the year. Food and football. What a wonderful combination! How can you go wrong? But it was during that holiday in 2005 that we would get our first glimpse that something wasn't right with Terry.

Our first indication that something was amiss came when he said that food that day didn't taste right. He complained that it didn't have much flavor. That was unusual for him, but I passed it off as being fatigued.

His first season at Indiana had just come to an end the week before, and we had lost the final six games to finish 4-7. The last game ended with a particularly lop-sided loss to Purdue in the annual Old Oaken Bucket game in Bloomington. So when he was a little irritable on Thanksgiving or borderline grumpy, as our son Drew recalled, we just figured it was leftover emotions from a season that had ended on a bad note. He was also starting to have headaches, but they were nowhere near the degree they would reach a month later.

Looking back, I remember thinking it was probably stress. I certainly never even considered that it could be brain cancer. There was no history of anything like that in his family. And anyone who knew him understood how fit and full of vigor he was. Whether it was golfing or swimming or running at football practice, he was always on the move. And so for him to have anything wrong took us all by surprise. Except for an arthritic hip, he was certainly not a person sickly in any way.

On December 17th the football staff had a Christmas progressive dinner that the wives had planned. The evening began with appetizers at Gerald and Jill Brown's house. We hosted the main course in our home and everyone finished the night at Bobby and Kristen Johnson's place. Again Terry had the same reaction to the smell and taste of food. Once more we passed it off as side effects of the season. In hindsight, many of the symptoms made sense. As one who looked forward to the turkey and dressing part of the holidays, his reaction was an early warning sign that something was not right.

Christmas that year was on Sunday. On Friday we traveled to Lebanon, Ohio, where our daughter Allison, her husband Drew and their boys Tate and Quinn lived. Our plan was to have our family gift exchange on Friday evening when our son Drew, daughter Amy, son-in-law Steve and boys Tucker and Spencer would join us. There was no time that Terry and I treasured more than being with our children and those four precious grandsons. The giving and receiving of gifts brought the desired reactions, especially one of Terry's presents. The kids gave him a Billy Cannon No. 20 LSU jersey. They knew that their dad had chosen 20 as his playing number because of his admiration for the former LSU running back. Hence for our family the number 20 will always hold a special significance.

On Saturday, Christmas Eve day, Terry, Drew and I headed to Cleveland for the Brown-Steelers game. We had been invited by Ben Roethlisberger, the Steelers quarterback who had played for us at Miami University. Terry was not feeling great, but we decided to make the trip anyway. Drew did the driving which allowed Terry to be more comfortable.

We arrived at the stadium and had a chance to visit with Ben on the field before the game. He and Terry shared a very special relationship, and it was good to see how well he was doing. It's very gratifying when one of your "guys" achieves what you knew was possible. Terry's expectations for Ben were being met and exceeded. For Drew to be able to share that day with us, made it even more meaningful. We watched the game from the press level and, while it was enjoyable (the Steelers won!), it was also very obvious that Terry wasn't up to speed.

Our trip back to Lebanon was similar to the early morning one — Drew driving and Terry trying to find a comfortable position. We stopped at a grocery store — finally finding one open — to get a few things I needed for our contribution to Christmas dinner the next day. Drew went in with me leaving Terry in the car, reclined, eyes closed, trying to relax. We got back to Allison's house late and planned to leave early the next morning for Cincinnati.

We arrived at Amy and Steve's house around 10 a.m., welcomed by those wonderful aromas of a Christmas feast being prepared. Once again Terry did not find the smell nearly as tantalizing and excused himself to lie down. I collected Tucker and Spencer, and we found a quiet place to finish *The Incredible Journey*. I had begun reading this book to them when they were visiting us in Bloomington and was determined to finish the "journey." Reading aloud to my third graders had been one my favorite parts of the school day. And it was no surprise that my grandsons, and I shared many adventures through the pages of a book. Just as we were enjoying the homecoming of the cat and two dogs, Terry appeared at the bedroom door. Before he spoke I knew what he was going to say. "We've got to go. We've got to go home."

Now obviously at that point there was a little bit of alarm. For him to want to leave on that particular day told me that this might be more than fatigue or stress. I thought we would go home and see a doctor, and he would be fine. Knowing him better than anyone else, there was no doubt in my mind that whatever the problem was would be remedied.

Thinking of a life-threatening condition wasn't even on the radar screen at that time. Still it wasn't something inconsequential either. Christmas is a big day in our family and the chance to spend it with our children and their families made it that much more special. Sadly, though, it was not something we were going to be able to do. We packed our things, said our good-byes and headed home to Bloomington.

It was a two and a half hour drive home with me behind the wheel and Terry reclined in the passenger seat. As I clutched the wheel, my heart was in my throat. I kept thinking when I was asking him how he felt that he would say he was doing better. But he never did. The headache had intensified to the point of making him nauseous which gave me a sense of urgency to get him home as quickly as possible. I remember being so intent on making the drive smooth and without too many bumps. I just didn't want him to be uncomfortable.

We arrived in Bloomington in late afternoon. We

were relieved to be out of the car and looked forward to the familiarity of home. Opening the door we were greeted by a freezing house, not at all the welcome we had anticipated. The furnace on the main floor was not working and this was one more unappreciated obstacle in an already trying day!

Because there was a separate system that heated the upstairs, he was able to go to bed in a warm room. As soon as he was situated, I called Dr. Andy Hipskind, one of our team doctors and family friend. I described Terry's symptoms, and he agreed that it must be serious if Coach was willing to leave his family in Cincinnati.

Andy told me he wanted to meet us at Bloomington Hospital at 10 a.m. the next morning. He said they would probably do a CT Scan to find out what was going on. When I told Terry, he was eager for the appointment to take place. He thought, as I did, that the scan would show a sinus infection or another less serious problem. We certainly weren't going to hear the words brain tumor. Now, was there somewhere in the back of my mind, where I thought that could be a possibility? Maybe. But our focus was getting to the doctor, getting some medicine and getting him feeling better.

We met Andy the next morning and proceeded to the radiology area. There was a feeling of inactivity in the hallways that was a reminder of the holiday season and people being with their loved ones on this day after Christmas. While Terry was undergoing the scan, I sat alone in the small waiting room. I prayed for Terry and those who were attending him. It wasn't long before they were finished and came to me with the results.

Something that had shown up in the x-ray needed to be further examined. An MRI was required for this more in depth look. The MRI proved to be more diffi-

cult than expected. There were two issues to deal with
— Terry's arthritic hip and the intense headache. Both
made it impossible for him to lie flat for a long period
of time. He got through the first part of it all right, but
then the pain became too much. He asked if I could go
into the room with him. Maybe by holding his hand
and squeezing it as a countdown, he could get through
the scan. It worked, and that's how we went through
every MRI he had. With the scan finally over, we
awaited word from the neurologist. The doctors agreed
that there appeared to be a tumor and surgery was
scheduled for the next morning. He was immediately
admitted to the hospital. Our 18-month journey had begun.

When one hears the words brain tumor, it causes a
profound reaction. Maybe shock would be most accu-
rate. I don't know. I do know that we were stunned.
There's a song called "Closer to Love" by Mat Kearney
that speaks about getting "that" phone call. Amy talks
about relating to that song. Each of our children got
that phone call from their dad, and they will never forget where they were or what they were doing when it
came.

Dr. Marshall Poor would be Terry's surgeon and
become his friend. From his first visit there was a bond
of trust between them. He and Terry traded stories and
shared a love of football. Terry enjoyed telling people
his brain surgeon was nicknamed Bubba. Really! He is
a gifted doctor blessed with a wonderful sense of humor. It was the perfect combination for us. He was exactly what we needed in our situation.

The night before his surgery was the beginning of
another "first" that would became a way of life for us.
He wanted me with him, and it was a good thing because I had already decided that we would be hospital
bunk mates! I got my fold-up bed in place and it felt

great to be beside each other. As we passed the evening a social worker came in with a form that needed to be filled out. One of the questions was, "Do you have a living will?" Terry smiled that smile of his and said, "I have a will to live and their names are Tucker, Spencer, Tate and Quinn."

After the volunteer left the room our conversation turned to the subject of texting. Terry had been making some calls and texting as well. I told him I had never received a text and wasn't sure I would know what to do if I did. This seems silly now, but at the time texting wasn't as commonplace as it is today. We laughed about it and then went back to what we were each reading.

About 30 minutes later a phone rang with an unfamiliar ring tone. I was puzzled and said, "Oh, my gosh, that's MY phone!" I opened it up and it was a text that said, "I love you." I looked up at him and there was that smile again. My very first text was from my best friend telling me in a brand new way that he loved me. Needless to say, I kept that text message.

From that first night in Bloomington Hospital there was a peace present in those times we spent together. We experienced it in that room on December 26th and in all the other places we would be over the next 18 months. I remember crawling into bed with him that night and snuggling a little bit and hoping we wouldn't get kicked out! But those were special moments.

We said the 23rd Psalm together as he was holding me close. It's a favorite psalm for many people because it speaks to things we face as we go through life. We all at some point will go through the valley of the shadow of death, but God is with us. He protects us and keeps us. It was for all those things we prayed together. We prayed that God would guide Dr. Poor's hands and that anyone who came into contact with Terry would do nothing to harm him. We felt very fortunate to have that time with each other. I'm not sure you always get the opportunity, but we did and we took advantage of it. We shared the time, and I was able to encourage him with the fact that "I'm not going anywhere!" All of that gave me such determination to stand firm and the willingness to be his protector. After all, he had, on occasion, done that for me.

I think back 20 years ago when we were living in Franklin. In the midst of raising children, taking classes and being a coach's wife, I made a startling discovery. Feeling what every woman dreads, there was a hard mass in my right breast. I said nothing about it at first, but it got worse and I made an appointment with our family physician, Dr. Reynolds. Terry was beside himself with worry. He asked, "Why would this happen to you?" In his mind he was thinking that this shouldn't happen to someone who is "good."

It was a period of introspection for both of us and a deepening of the relationship that we shared. I knew without a doubt that he would take my place in a heartbeat. And 20 years later he knew that I would have done the same for him. At that point I hadn't said anything to my parents, but Terry suggested I call them right then. My father and mother were strong believers in the power of prayer along with many friends who shared their view.

After my checkup with Dr. Reynolds, he immediately scheduled me to see a surgeon at the hospital. That morning as I showered there seemed to be a change in the hardness. Or was it my imagination? We got to the hospital where I was checked in. and I was taken to the dressing room to don the gown. I looked out and saw Terry standing there with that expression on his face of total helplessness. He was the one who could fix problems, but there was nothing he could do now except stand there.

I was taken to a surgical room where I was examined. After much poking and prodding, the doctor said, "There's nothing here. I'm not sure why you're here." Whatever had been there was gone! I was in awe at that moment and so grateful to God for prayers answered in such a way.

When I left the dressing room and found Terry, he was talking to Dr. Reynolds. He had come to the hospital because he thought we would be receiving a bad report from the specialist. The doctors had no explanations, but it served as a wake-up call for both of us. We would NEVER take our time together for granted. It was the same way I felt as we lay in the hospital bed the night before his surgery. How blessed we were as a couple to have those awesome moments to share.

Our children all arrived at some time that evening and were at the hospital early the next morning. It was an unsettling time. Dealing with the unknown can be frightening. But from the beginning we leaned hard on God. We prayed fervently and knew that family and friends all over the country were joining with us.

The nurses and doctors took care of all the pre-op procedures and it was time for him to be taken away. We had kissed and whispered all those last minute encouragements to each other. And then as they are wheeling him away, we heard his last words: "Did they fix the furnace?" Even under medication, he was making sure everything at home was all right!

Amy, Allison, Drew and I headed for the little waiting room to pass the time until we got word from Dr. Poor. What would I have done without family? We told stories, laughed, prayed, made phone calls and waited.

After several hours we answered the knock at the door and listened to what Bubba had to say. Things had gone well and it looked like they got it all. We all embraced and began making more phone calls. After spending some time in recovery, Terry was taken to intensive care. Once again a bed had been provided for me and I was able to be beside him. The kindnesses shown to us were too many to count. I will always be thankful for the nurses and doctors that took such good care of both of us.

The day after surgery Dean Kleinschmidt, our football trainer, stopped by to check up on Terry and found him drawing up plays. In his mind he was back at work and talking football. He may have been in ICU, but it wasn't going to slow him down. I remember people being surprised by that, but I wasn't. That was vintage Coach Hep. It was with this very same attitude that we approached life after his first surgery. We were convinced that he was going to beat this. It was the way we thought and lived. He was going to beat it, and one day he would have a great story to tell.

Because Terry and I had always been avid readers, people may have assumed that we would research everything about brain cancer in general and specifically the type Terry had. Actually that wasn't the case at all. Not for me anyway. Terry may have done it and I didn't know, but I never read a word about it. I didn't research it on the Internet or read books about it. Many people would have immediately been at the computer trying to find information. But that wasn't my way.

I'm sure some would call that denial, but we were so determined to move through this time in a positive manner. I didn't want to give worry a place in my thoughts. And while it was a battle I didn't always win, there were enough victories to encourage me to keep trusting — not worrying. Whichever of those you choose to nurture will be the one to grow. I tried to feed the trust and starve the worry. It's not that I didn't understand the seriousness of the situation or the possible outcome, but I did have a choice as to my outlook. We sold out to believing that things would work out for our good. We sought God and didn't turn away from Him even though there were times when it seemed quiet.

Even though there were moments when I had questions, we probably all did, there remained an underlying peace that was such a firm foundation for Terry and me. There may be people who will read this and think that we were being naïve and didn't grasp the magnitude of what Terry was up against. But that wasn't it at all.

My dad, Paul Madinger, was sent home from the hospital with hospice in January of 2002. He was 79 years old. After having open heart surgery, he struggled coming out from under the anesthetic. Eventually he did, and all of his organs were functioning except his kidneys. Because he couldn't tolerate dialysis, the doctors said they had done all they could do.

He was sent home on a Sunday with instructions on how to keep him comfortable. My brother, Paul, sister, Barbara and I helped our mother with what looked like our dad's last days. But in the midst of this, his kidneys began to function. My brother-in-law, who is an internist, felt something could be done for him and knew of a colleague who specialized in older, critically ill patients.

On Thursday Charles arrived, and he and Barbara transported our dad to Mobile and admitted him to a hospital there. Somehow he pulled through. And he's still alive today. For our family and for Terry, we have seen someone who was given no hope make a complete recovery. We were witnesses to it.

That experience undoubtedly colored our perception toward life-threatening illnesses. That, on some level, was a faith-builder. All of our life experiences come into play when we have to face adversity. They affect our attitude one way or the other, and in our case they helped us keep a positive outlook.

3

The Battle is On

After Terry's first surgery our journey was well underway. Our lives were changing by the minute. One of the first decisions we had to make when Terry got out of intensive care was what our next course of action would be. How were we going to fight the cancer?

One option that presented itself was proton therapy. The location of the tumor seemed to suggest that this was the best plan of attack. Proton therapy is a very precise procedure that provides a high level of radiation to an exact target. At that time, only three locations in the United States offered this type of treatment: Boston, Mass., Loma Linda, Calif., and Bloomington, Ind. And the location of the last one was across the street from Memorial Stadium!

Midwest Proton Radiotherapy Institute (MPRI) seemed liked the answer we were looking for. Late one night after what we would come to find out was a "normal" day for him, Dr. Alan Thornton came to see us at the hospital. His explanation was very thorough and he patiently listened to our concerns and answered our questions. We decided at that time that proton therapy was the first treatment we would try.

Terry never really kept a journal or diary, but at the time of his first surgery he did jot down some thoughts and reactions about what was happening to him. He recorded these notes in the weeks leading up to the start of proton therapy in early February.

He envisioned writing a book someday that would chronicle his fight and ultimate victory over brain cancer. The first entry was the day before his surgery. "When principles and core beliefs are tested, when everything you've learned and practiced is exposed and examined ... can you believe, truly believe, what you've been preaching your entire adult life? When you are given a chance to really make a difference, do you?"

That same day he also jotted down some of his favorite sayings, "Have a plan, work the plan and plan for the unexpected." He added, "It was third and long, but Coach Hep got a miracle and a fresh set of downs." The last notation was a verse from Romans. "If God is for you, who can be against you?"

I found his book soon after he died and put it away for safekeeping. It stayed in that drawer until I began gathering material for this book. I wept as I opened it up and saw his handwriting. In that powerful moment, it felt as though he were speaking to me and giving me a priceless gift!

Upon returning home from the hospital one of his entries read: "Thank you that I am healed. The potter sometimes breaks the vase and starts over." Below that it said, "Our God is an awesome God" and "Trust and obey."

Christians everywhere speak of being born again (John 3:7). I believe Terry had that kind of experience on the night of January 5, 2006, and it would forever change him. He had an encounter in the middle of the night, and when he woke up the next morning he was different. That's the best way to say it — he was not the same.

In his journal he wrote, "Last night was the greatest night of my life. This is the best thing that every happened to me. No compromise. My life will never be the same. How I coach, how I feel about the game. Last night I stopped negotiating with God. He hit me right in the mouth (or brain!). I can't wait for the future. We will win, but doing our best is the new goal. John Wooden understood." (He had recently finished a book about Coach Wooden.)

Later that morning as we drove to IU Medical Center in Indianapolis, he talked to me about it. He said there would be no more negotiating. He said he had tried to work things out his whole life, trying to manipulate things to work out the way he wanted. Somehow that night he got a glimpse of the awesomeness of God.

I don't know what that looked like, but it shook him to the core. It really did. It impacted the way he thought and in turn the way he lived from that day forward. I remember him calling our kids and telling them about it as well. From that day on he referred to January 5th as his second birthday.

There were also various snippets in his journal that referred to what he was thinking and doing. "Slept well for six hours. Up at five. Wrote a letter to the HT (*The Herald Times* newspaper in Bloomington). Feel good. Another great day. Got scholarship numbers straight. IU 81-OSU 79. Watched NFL game in the evening. Felt even better today."

And there was a scripture from Joshua that read, "As for me and my house, we will serve the Lord." We began to study the Bible and agreed that we desired to have a better understanding of the history as well as the message. We found among our books one called *Thirty Days To Understanding the Bible*. It was a look at the overall themes as well as a book by book indepth analysis. It was exactly what we needed.

This period of recovery was providing us with time for introspection and appreciation for each other. We had stopped to smell the roses. His journal entry said it perfectly. "My spirit is healed, and my body is healing."

I, as well as Terry, was spending time recording thoughts and scriptures that were especially meaningful to me. Jeremiah 29:11 became our family's favorite verse, and we all quickly knew it by heart. "'For I know the plans I have for you,' says the Lord. 'Plans to prosper you and not to harm you, plans to give you a hope and a future.'"

I thought God's plan involved everything going back to the way it was for us. Sometimes I would write down observations of Terry as he continued to persevere. "Terry was up from 2:30-3:30 working on football personnel. He gets lots accomplished in the night. God continues to give us His peace. He knows what we need before we even think of it. Sometimes in the wee hours God impresses on me that what we need now he has already taken care of. Jesus took on all our infirmities and was victorious over them. He is able to do what we cannot do. It was a debt we had no ability or means to pay. What can compare to the awesomeness of God?"

January of 2006 was a time of healing and making preparations for the proton therapy treatments that would begin in February. The start date was moved back a week so we could attend the Super Bowl in Detroit on Feb 5th. Ben Roethlisberger, our quarterback who Terry had recruited and coached at Miami University, was in the championship game.

His success with the Pittsburgh Steelers was no surprise to us and we were not going to miss the chance to see him play in the Big Game! Several procedures had to be completed before Terry was ready for the proton therapy. Because of the preciseness of the treatment, patients must have tiny BBs implanted as points of reference. This outpatient surgery was done on January 16th. My journal read, "Today was Terry's implant surgery. Saturday night before we went to sleep, we prayed for guidance as we took this next step. Is this the way to go?? Today when we went to the hospital, we were admitted to outpatient surgery. The nurses took Terry's vitals and gave him the hospital gown. As he walked out of the room the nurse said, 'By the way you are in room 20.' We smiled at each other and shook our heads in amazement. The number 20 is a special one for our family, and God knew we would understand that. It was the most incredibly, perfectly timed message from the One who was watching over us."

The next step in preparation was a procedure called mapping.

This involved calculating the trajectory of the beam so it would meet its desired target. It addition to the scans taken for the mapping, Terry had to be fitted for a mouthpiece and face mask. These would ensure that there was no movement during treatment.

We learned that there would be five treatments a week for 10 weeks. They were scheduled from February 7th to April 14th. We also learned a few other things about how he was progressing. My journal entry: "We're at MPRI having our consult. We've done check-in and medical history, and we're waiting to see Dr. Thornton. Great news from the CT scan on Tuesday. No tumor and the brain looks relaxed. Good blood flow that was not there pre-op. We actually looked at the scans before and after surgery. God is faithful and continues to give us his peace and mercy."

January was also the time that Terry began returning to his duties at the office. Although he was working daily on football at home, he felt the need to be back at his desk. On January 9th he began easing into his return. He would stay for several hours and that was his routine for the next few weeks.

On January 15th we made a surprise appearance at the Football Awards Banquet. It was important to him to be able to thank everyone for their love and support. Being in the midst of friends and colleagues certainly buoyed our spirits and we hoped it had the same impact on them.

The first Wednesday in February is National Signing Day for college football and always an exciting (and sometimes anxious!) time for coaching staffs all over the country. On February 1st we signed a great class and looked forward to watching them mature as players and men. New beginnings bring with them a sense of promise, and this happens each year when players choose to spend the next four or five years as a part of your program.

The following Friday we left for Super Bowl XL in Detroit. We were so pleased to be able to spend time with Ben and his family after the game at the hotel victory celebration. It seemed like only yesterday that Ken and Brenda were bringing their son for his recruiting visit to Miami. We marveled at how Ben's life was unfolding and were grateful for how his parents had raised him.

From the excitement and hoopla of the Super Bowl we headed back to Bloomington where the unknown once again awaited us. My journal entry on February 7th: "… the armor of God: truth, righteousness, the gospel of peace, faith , salvation, the Word. Ephesians 6:10-

20. We need God's protection today. Yesterday we heard all about the side effects of proton therapy, and it was disheartening. But I refuse to bow my knee to fear, and I declare that greater is he who is in me than he that is in the world. I won't bow my knee to the fear of the unknown. Today I choose to believe God's Word."

My February 10th entry: "Our first week of treatment is almost over. Forty-seven to go. We have been blessed by the kind people that work at MPRI. We are very thankful for them." On most days Terry's treatment time was 3:45 p.m. and because it only took about 30 minutes, he would usually return to the office when he was finished. I went with him and was able to sit in a room and watch the procedure on the monitor.

We had another one of those No. 20 experiences during one of his treatments. He said he didn't know how many times he had been in that room and stared up at the ceiling and hadn't seen it. But on this particular day I noticed that he kept his eyes open longer, and I was curious as to why. As we were leaving he said the inscription on the machine said Motoman 20. For anyone else it wouldn't mean a thing, but for us it was like a much appreciated hug from God.

On Saturday February 11th Terry spoke at halftime of the IU-Iowa basketball game at Assembly Hall. He received a thunderous ovation. This was my journal entry that day: "Terry is speaking at halftime at the basketball game today. It will be so encouraging for the fans as well as to us. God has been so gracious to us. His word is true. It's all we need." February 13th: "Terry's halftime talk was a rousing and roaring success! Everyone was thrilled to see him. It was hard getting out afterward. We watched the second half in his office."

It felt good to be in a familiar routine again. Terry was planning for spring ball and had resumed speaking engagements. There was some fatigue, but he proved to be an expert at power napping! We celebrated when he had his last treatment on March 30th.

Shortly after this milestone of sorts, the doctors told us that everything on the follow-up scan looked good. It was pretty obvious that my husband had not lost his sense of humor. When the doctors gave him the news, one went so far as to say it was perfect. Another said he was great and a third said he was much better. In a story that spring in the *Indianapolis Star* Terry was quoted as saying, "So I'm somewhere between much better and perfect. When the doctor said perfect, I said 'Wow! That's a lot better than I was before the surgery!'"

The transformation that had begun in Terry at the beginning of the year continued and manifested itself in many ways. The further we went in our journey, the clearer I saw the changes in him. Most notably he looked for chances to reach out to others and help them in some way.

He thoroughly enjoyed bringing 'Coach Hep' gear to the son of Chris, our MRI technician. He might bring a hat, a T-shirt, or an IU schedule poster or media guide. We learned all about her son's talent as a golfer and that endeared him to Terry at once. Corrie, the medical assistant to Dr. Dropcho at the Medical Center, also had a son who was the recipient of Hoosier memorabilia. It was a special visit when she shared the poem with us that her son Zach had written about Coach Hep. They even joined us in Bloomington for a game. We were grateful for these people who were a part of our lives even for a brief time. We were finding that it wasn't about us. God's plan was much bigger than that.

Around this time Terry and I first heard Martina McBride sing her new song, "Anyway," on a music awards program. As one of our favorite artists, we were both listening closely to the lyrics and enjoying her voice. When she finished the song we both had the same reaction. Wow! The words were a call to do the right thing regardless of what the outcome might be. For us it became an instant favorite. It was also an obvious and bittersweet choice when it was used with one of the videos at his memorial service.

As our faith walk grew, Terry and I both realized that there were areas in our lives that needed to be addressed and made right. For me one of those was an incident that had occurred over 20 years earlier when we were living in South Carolina.

I ordered flowers to be placed on the altar on our last Sunday as a farewell gesture. We left town the next morning headed for Indiana. In the chaos of moving, the bill for the flowers was delayed in reaching us. When it did arrive, time had elapsed and it just didn't get paid. The more time that passed, the less urgency I felt about paying it.

Finally, I was able to rationalize it completely and that was that. Or so it seemed. I was able to put it out of my mind except when I would begin to pray. And then I was reminded of it. This scenario had gone on for years. When I was still, the thought would come into my mind — you didn't pay that person.

And so on one of those quiet evenings following Terry's surgery, I slipped to the computer and looked up the florist's name. There were two listings and I copied down both addresses. Next I composed two letters in which I apologized and asked for forgiveness for my selfishness and irresponsibility. I put money and a letter in each envelope and sealed them. I then proceeded to the family room where my husband was reading in his recliner and explained to him what I had done. He knew nothing about it because I had never spoken of it. But it was on my conscience, and I couldn't get away from that.

Many times I talked the good talk, but I needed to

be obedient with this and do what was right. I had always rationalized that it was not a big deal, but none of that washed and God saw through it all. I remember Terry's surprised and pleased reaction and I found that by sharing our shortcomings with each other, the bond between us was made even stronger.

This is an example of what happened for us when we got serious about how we were living our lives. And how we live involves not just our thoughts and intentions, but what we actually **DO**. This is how we live out our faith. For me this revelation was awesome. That night when I went to bed and closed my eyes to pray, there was never again that reminder of a debt that needed to be paid!

When I look back on the road we traveled together, the miracle for us was the work that God did in our hearts. It would have been amazing for Terry's story to be that "I had this cancer and now it's gone. I'm going to pick up where I left off."

But that was not what happened. Everyone's body is going to wear out. The blind man that Jesus healed eventually died. The spirit within us is the living part of who we are even though we cannot see it. It does not die with the body. God taught us that the real fight is for the heart and who is on the throne of that heart. The spiritual battle proved to be the more important of the two.

4

He Refused to Quit

For our family, summer has always been a season that we looked forward to with great anticipation. As a teacher I shared with my students the excitement of having a break from the daily classroom routine. I can still recall waking up as a child and remembering that it was the first day of summer vacation. Since I was one of four children, my mother may have had a different reaction!

The expectations for the summer of 2006 were much the same as in previous years. Terry was in the office until July when he would take some vacation time, but the long days of sunlight provided time for rounds of golf, jet-skiing at Lake Monroe and playing in the pool.

Allison and her husband Drew had moved to Bloomington in April, and we enjoyed them daily. Terry was the perfect grandfather for Tucker, Spencer, Tate and Quinn. He never lost his boyish love of play, and now he had four little people who reveled in his love and attention.

Early on the morning of Friday, June 30th, we got a call from Bobby Johnson, one of our coaches. Bobby had played for us at Miami and eventually became part of our staff. He and Kristen were like family to us. He said, "Randy's gone." I asked him to repeat it. I couldn't understand what he was saying. I handed the phone to Terry not wanting to believe what I had heard. Randy Walker, our close friend and coaching colleague, had experienced heart failure the night before and passed away.

Randy and Terry were friends beyond the confines of football. They were golfing buddies who loved discussing everything from books to politics to life in general. We had been together 10 years at Miami before Randy left to take the Northwestern job. He had left the defensive coordinator's spot open in case Terry would accept the offer to join him, but the head position at Miami was what Terry wanted. Randy gave his blessing and recommendation on his behalf to athletic director Joel Maturi.

It seemed impossible that he was gone. We called his wife Tammy immediately and made plans to head to Evanston, Ill. The service could not be held until the following Friday because their daughter Abbey and her husband were living in Paris and there was travel time involved. She was also expecting a baby, Randy and Tammy's first grandchild.

Terry was asked to speak at the service and later told me that it was the hardest thing he had ever done. I found the notes that he used when he gave his tribute to his friend. The similarities to what would be said a year later about Terry were stunning. He recalled his thoughts of Randy: His love for Tammy, Abbey and Jamie, the Circle of Walk — all those impacted by his life, Walk's magic fingers — an inside joke that brought laughter from former players. He talked about Randy's stock response of "I'm doin' great." He said that we are all a part of his legacy and that Randy was gone too soon. He ended with the mantra that they both shared, "It's how you respond." The word respond was underlined several times. "You taught us well, Walk. We will respond. Job well done."

We drove back to Bloomington with heavy hearts, but knew that Tammy was surrounded by a strong group of family and friends. Her first grandchild, Clara, was born the next November and brought with her the gift of life and a new beginning. A brother would follow, Walker Randolph. Randy would be so proud!

Our return home was brightened by the arrival of our son, Drew, and Amy and Steve and their boys. We had a birthday to celebrate — Tate was turning six. We enjoyed a day on the water at Lake Monroe and felt the rejuvenating effect that family had on us.

August brought with it Big Ten meetings, family visits, more birthdays and more MRIs. Three of the four were good. My sister, Barbara, and her daughters, Bethany and Dorothy, drove up from Alabama and stayed for almost a week. We took the girls on what we called the Indy Tour — driving by our childhood homes, schools, church, etc. and capturing it all on camera. Our parents enjoyed it vicariously when we called them to ask for addresses of their early haunts. Terry's mother, Phyllis, came to visit next. She and Tucker share the same birthday right in between Quinn's and Terry's. There was lots of gift giving for us in August.

Terry and I had attended the Big Ten meetings in Chicago at the first of the month. There was a routine scan done the day after we returned. Freshmen players reported on the 5th, so preseason practice was underway. The scan had shown something that the doctors didn't like, and we met with Dr. Thornton about the possibility of doing proton therapy again. He resumed treatment and looked forward to the challenge of preparing his team for a successful season. The weekly routine was once again in place — staff meetings, practice, press conferences, radio show, watching tape and game planning.

Our season opened with a win over Western Michigan University. We were off to a good start. The next Friday Terry had an MRI, but was focused on facing Ball State the next day. It was a rainy, ugly slug fest, with the Hoosiers prevailing, 24-23.

On Monday we met with Bubba about the results of the scan. It was hard to tell what was happening because after brain surgery there can be scar tissue that shows up. We agreed that we should go in and have it taken care of. It was a touchy procedure because of the location near the spine, and there's always a chance of doing harm to something else. It was a risk, but one we needed to take.

We had confidence in Bubba's opinion and so that's what we opted to do. On that day, September 11, I wrote: "God will never leave us or forsake us. We trust Him with our lives. We will not fear. God hasn't given us a spirit of fear, but of power and love and a sound mind. Guide our hearts, guide our thoughts and words as we go through this time. Thank you for the joy you give and the peace. Help us to be a blessing to those we will be with. Guide the hands of all those who touch Terry. Let nothing be done to him that is not completely OK with you. Prepare the nurses and doctors to be positive and not negative." I wrote this on a card that I had received from my friend Bevo Muehling. She was so good at sending cards at just the right time. It must have been the only thing I could find to write on.

The next day, shortly after Terry had told his team that he was going to have a second brain surgery, he called a press conference at Memorial Stadium. With his friend and confidante Rick Greenspan beside him, he announced that he was having surgery the next day at Bloomington Hospital.

I've never been more proud of him than I was at that moment. He was responding to a "bad call" that wouldn't be overturned and was doing it with class, teary eyes and that awesome smile. We were surprised by the number of people who had taken the time to come, John and Elaine Mellencamp among them. We had attended a Fourth of July party at their home and had especially enjoyed their sons, Hud and Speck. They were in charge of the fireworks, and they put on quite a show.

I had called Anthony Thompson and asked if he and Lori could meet with us afterwards. Anthony was well known to Indiana fans as a former IU All-American running back. He continued on as an assistant football coach and later took a position with the Varsity Club. Anthony also served as pastor of Lighthouse Community Church in Bloomington. He and Terry had made a connection first through athletics, and later on a deeper level. We looked forward to his visits to our home when he would encourage us to keep the faith. On this day there was no doubt that we wanted A.T. standing with us. We went into Terry's office and talked about what was ahead. They prayed with us and we were at peace with what we had to face the next day.

We were up early the next morning, packed and ready for a 7 a.m. admittance time. Our son, Drew, had surprised his dad and arrived during his radio show on Monday night. We were glad to have him drop us off at a side door when we realized there were television trucks and reporters at the main entrance.

Kelly, Dr. Poor's surgical nurse, oversaw the pre-op details and gave us another opportunity to tease her about her allegiance to the University of Kentucky.

She, like so many others, had become a family favorite. When Terry was ready, we said our goodbyes and were taken to a waiting room to watch the clock and pray. Allison had arrived, as well as several family friends, and we shared tears and laughter together.

When the operation was over, Terry was once again in ICU and began talking about football when he came out from under the anaesthetic. It had been a long day for everyone and so I was especially touched when Kelly and Bubba stopped by later that evening and handed me a card and gift bag. That day, September 13th, was my birthday, and they had given me two books and a card on which they had signed Terry's name! It was a birthday I'll never forget.

On Friday of that week, two days after Terry's surgery, the Indiana Board of Trustees was meeting to hear a presentation about plans for athletic facility improvements. A large part of that plan was a renovation of Memorial Stadium that would include enclosing the north end zone as well as creating office space, team rooms and a much-needed area for weight training. This was a topic that was very dear to Terry and part of his vision for Indiana football.

So two days after surgery there was no doubt in his mind where he needed to be. As the meeting began, Terry and I entered from the back of the room and found seats near the front. It was an emotional moment for us and for all who were there that day.

Of course, my husband couldn't stop with just making a presentation at the board meeting. He was also determined to be at Saturday's game against Southern Illinois. The doctors weren't keen about him going, but we found a way that seemed like it would work.

Jimmie and Curt Durnil were the Indiana State Troopers assigned to Terry's security detail. In December of 2004, they were the first people we met when we got off the plane in Bloomington. They escorted us to the president's office for a brief meeting and then to Memorial Stadium for Terry's first press conference as the Indiana coach. And now they were escorting us once again. They came to our house and took us to the stadium where we were dropped off at the elevator that went to the press box.

He went to the coaches' box, and I headed to our family's box with blood pressure monitor in tow just in case. The coaches may have been a little surprised to see him, but then again probably not. Terry was very competitive and very stubborn. For him to have been away from the game, even for a weekend, would have been impossible.

At halftime when the coaches went to the locker room, I took him a plate of food and tested his blood pressure. His vitals were fine, but his state of mind was not great. He wanted to be with his guys, not watching them. When the game ended we were whisked home the same way we had gotten there. We did the same routine the next Saturday, and the week after that he was on the sidelines coaching in the Big Ten opener against Wisconsin.

In his press conference before the Wisconsin game, Terry talked about his second surgery. He told everyone that "Jane got scar tissue for her birthday." We were hopeful that this was the case and excited about being back with the team and staff.

We were also excited because the Steelers had a bye week, and Ben would be coming for the game. Even though his visit was short, we enjoyed having him in our home. That was definitely the highlight of the weekend. Terry was not happy that we had lost the game. The season's bright spots were wins over Iowa and Michigan State. We got an added bonus on the day we beat the Spartans. The Beach Boys were in concert at the IU Auditorium that evening and Terry got to perform "Be True to your School" with them. As a lifelong fan he was thrilled!

As the season wore on, I could see my best friend becoming more and more fatigued. He was on medication and that may have contributed to it as well. Coaching a football team requires a high level of energy under normal circumstances. And to go through a season battling brain cancer was quite a challenge. Because I was with him every step of the way, my perspective was very subjective. Someone who was only seeing him once a week or less often may have seen a more dramatic change in the way he was beginning to look. But because I was right here in the moment, it was just different for me.

Thanksgiving was upon us as soon as the season was finished. It was at this time that Winkle joined us. As we were making preparations in the kitchen, Tate announced that there was a cat on the deck. Sure enough there was a tiny gray and white cat standing at the door. My first words were, "Don't feed it!" But of course we did. Tate gave her a saucer of milk and that was all it took for him to think that she belonged to us. His two-year old brother, Quinn, while looking eye to eye through the sliding door at our visitor, shouted to me, "Mim, that cat just winkled at me!" And so the name Winkle seemed to be the perfect fit.

We kept her as an outside cat and managed to stop being appalled at the "gifts" she insisted on leaving at our door. After Terry passed away Tate told me that he had a question for God when he got to heaven. I braced myself for the deep, theological query and asked what he wanted to know. His answer, "Where **DID** Winkle come from?" Hugging him tight, I said I've wondered the same thing!

December was a busy time with recruiting visits,

addressing end-of-year academic matters and meeting with players. All of our kids would be home for Christmas, and we were looking forward to that. Terry was continuing to rest whenever possible. He would stretch out in his office after lunch and grab a nap. Or if he had come home, he would use his recliner before he went back to work.

January brought with it the National Football Coaches Association Convention in San Antonio, as well as some speaking engagements. Our time in Texas was one of seeing many old friends and faces. We enjoyed being together and walking along the River Walk. It seemed odd that Tammy and Randy weren't there.

Once again the February National Signing Day was upon us. I could see that Terry's stamina was pretty low. His assistants helped out with the press conference and talked about the recruiting class. It was hard to see him not be able to enjoy what was one of his favorite days as a coach: welcoming a new group of student athletes.

The rest of the month was filled with obligations that he was determined to keep. We went to Las Vegas for an Adidas Convention where he had to do a presentation. Our activities were limited because of his need to rest. We ate out several times and did a little shopping, but took our time.

We returned on Sunday the 18th. Terry was scheduled to speak on Tuesday in Cincinnati at the Football Foundation Dinner, at an IUPUI function Friday morning and receive the Terry Cole Courage Award at the Football Foundation Dinner at the Colts Complex in Indianapolis on Saturday.

The following week he spoke at the NCAA Hall of Champions luncheon in Indianapolis. We didn't realize it at the time, but that would be his last public appearance.

During this time we celebrated our 39th wedding anniversary and chuckled at Allison's thoughtful and well-placed greetings. She had made copies of an old picture of us when we were students at Franklin. She then put them all over the house! I kept finding them days later, and it made the celebration last a little longer.

Terry's thoughts were of getting re-energized for spring football, but that wasn't to be. In March the press release read, "He needed time to regain his strength and energy and to receive proper medical care."

He refused to quit.

5

"I Couldn't Be
Me Without You"

In April of 2007 we decided that Terry might benefit from some type of physical therapy. As one who had always made fitness a priority, he was frustrated by his weakened condition. We felt that engaging the services of a professional who could come to our home would be beneficial.

While I believed this was the right course of action, there was also some apprehension about having a stranger in our house. We had recently had a visitor who insisted on seeing Terry and was reluctant to leave without getting to talk to him. I had become much more forceful in handling uncomfortable situations and had no problem ending the conversation by closing the door. Because of this experience, I called our lawyer, who is a long-time family friend, and asked if he could draw up a type of confidentiality/background agreement.

Once again I prayed for guidance and wisdom in

this situation. Bloomington Hospital provided me with a name, and I initiated contact with the therapist, Eddie Getts. He would prove to be the next person to make a perfectly-timed appearance into our lives.

Coach and Eddie had quite a mutual admiration society. He was an avid IU football fan and had followed our story. During one of their discussions, they figured out that their paths had crossed years earlier. Eddie had attended one of the Bishop Dullaghan Summer Passing Camps when he was in high school. Terry had worked those camps every summer as they were held at Franklin College.

We soon realized that the values he held were the same ones that Terry and I espoused. He would visit several times a week with a regimen of exercises that we hoped would improve Terry's strength.

There was a variety of stretching activities that were to be completed daily in addition to physical therapy days. We got to know one another during these sessions, and we were especially touched by Eddie's involvement in foster care. He and his wife had such hearts for children and put their faith into action by adopting four little ones.

We found that Eddie was an active outdoorsman and sports enthusiast. Boating, biking, hiking, pretty much any outing that involved fresh air and a physical challenge interested him. It was not a surprise then that he chose a quiet, solitary place in the woods for his time alone with God.

It was at this spot one day where he was praying intently for Coach. While in the midst of this, he noticed a large geode that was broken into two pieces. For those unfamiliar with the geology of southern Indiana, a geode is a bumpy, brown rock that resembles a clump of dirt. However, when broken apart, it contains thousands of sparkling crystals.

For some reason he thought of Terry when he looked at it. He picked up one half of the rock and the other he left in place as a reminder of his friend. It became literally a touch-stone for him. The other half of the geode he gave to us. It helped Terry and me remember the faithful people who were standing with us in this battle.

A couple of weeks after Terry died, Eddie stopped by the house. He had called ahead to make sure I would be home, and I looked forward to hearing all of the Getts family news. But his purpose in visiting that day was more than a social call. When I opened the door to welcome him, I immediately saw the reason he had come.

He was holding the other half of the geode. I went to the study and brought back the rock that had been given to us. When we put them together we marveled at how the two pieces became whole once more. We both knew Coach had been made whole again as well. This stone, that provided such a life lesson for me, remains in a place where I can see it daily and smile at the thought of our friend, Eddie Getts.

The month of May brought increased periods of sleeping for Terry and a voice that became much weaker. Terry also had bouts with the hiccups that his doctors thought may have been brought on by his medication. Regardless of the cause, they were a dreaded occurrence that left him even more exhausted. Somehow we stumbled onto a remedy that we found sometimes worked — drinking Fresca! This came after we tried drinking water in every position possible, taking teaspoons of sugar and holding his breath.

He didn't seem to be talking as much, but his spirits remained upbeat. We had few visitors, but each one was special and had a meaningful purpose in our journey. Our friend Anthony Thompson came regularly to encourage us and pray with us. He would occasionally bring his friend/colleague, Pastor David Beecham. Their kindness to our family will never be forgotten. They understood our position of refusing to give up and stood boldly in the gap for us. Their visits were instrumental in helping us to sustain our positive outlook. They fueled our spirits and kept our minds focused on the source of our strength in this fight.

During the treatment that Terry was receiving at this time, regular blood draws were required to make sure his counts were high enough. The nurse who was assigned to do this at our office visit had difficulty finding a good spot. After several attempts, I said no more. Either we would have to find someone who could do it or we were finished with the draws. Knowing the importance of the procedure, I prayed that God would send the right person soon.

The next day we returned and waited for the person they had found to try doing the draw. In came Marilyn who very quietly went about finding the best vein on her first try. As she was gathering up her equipment to leave, she confessed how nervous she had been and that she had prayed in her car on the way. She asked for God's help and we assured her that she had most certainly been an answer to our prayers.

Marilyn would continue coming to our home for blood draws and she never failed to get a good stick on the first attempt. Her expertise was so helpful, and we loved her gentle nature. Because of our family's affection for her, I was surprised that we didn't hear from her after Terry passed away.

Later that fall I got a phone call and immediately recognized Marilyn's voice. It was wonderful to hear from her and find that she was doing well. When I told her that I missed hearing from her earlier, she told me that she didn't think I would remember her! She had completely underestimated the value we placed on her friendship and the important role she had played in our lives. None of us will ever forget Marilyn Philpott.

As I look at my May 2007 calendar, I see MRI appointments, blood draw dates, doctor's visits, jotted observations of Terry's condition, and I'm reminded by the handwriting in some of the entries that I had a consistent and faithful companion through all of the long and sometimes difficult days.

We were blessed that Allison and her family were nearby and able to essentially move in with us and help me with the day to day chore of fighting the fight. When I see her handwriting on those calendar entries, I remember her sacrifice and how, in spite of the circumstances, it was a special time.

Special times like May 29 where she wrote, "Serenaded Mom — Johnny Rodriquez." "I Couldn't Be Me Without You" is an old, little remembered ballad that Terry had dubbed "our song." The words to it, while rather corny, expressed his feelings for me and mine for him. Terry had an incredible memory and knew the words to hundreds of songs. He loved music of all kinds, but was partial to country. While he wasn't always on key, he never got the lyrics wrong! And he had my full attention that Tuesday evening in 2007 when he began singing our song. What his voice lacked in strength, was more than made up for in the depth of love I saw in his eyes.

Along with the weakness he was experiencing, Terry was beginning to have trouble with congestion. On the first Sunday in June, Dr. Lori Thompson, (A.T.'s wife) stopped by to check on him. She was there a short time and it was determined that he needed to go to the hospital.

We would be there for 13 days, and I recorded many of my thoughts and reactions as we walked through the valley. I found myself being a hospital roommate once more and we passed the time in quiet companionship. Well, part of the time anyway, between visits from doctors and hourly checks by nurses. Dr. Poor came in each day just to say hello and make sure Coach was behaving himself. It always brought a smile to Terry's face.

My journal entries contain many scriptures that reveal the mindset that we continued to have.

On June 5th there are seven verses listed, beginning with, "God has not given us a spirit of fear, but of power and love and a sound mind." The last entry says, "All things work together for good to those who love God and are called according to his purpose."

The next day Drew came to visit with the news that he was interviewing with an airline for a position as a commercial pilot. It was also the day Beth, our hospital physical therapist, came into the room and introduced herself. She leaned over Terry and asked, "How do you want me to address you? Coach?" He said to her in a whisper, "Your Excellency." We all burst out laughing! Through everything he had been through, he hadn't lost his great sense of humor and his impeccable timing.

June 7th — "This is the day the Lord has made. We will rejoice and be glad in it." I wrote about how much we had grown through this process and how God had revealed Himself to us in so many ways and through so many people. I recalled the peace that was present in room 4507. Pastor Beecham visited that afternoon and prayed with us.

June 9th — Jeremiah 9:24 "But let him who glories glory in this: that he understands and knows me, that I am the Lord, who practices loving kindness, judgment and righteousness in the earth, for in these things I delight," says the Lord. I spoke with Dr. Larry Rink concerning Terry's condition and what preparations needed to be set in motion before he could go home.

June 10th — II Corinthians 1:3-5 "Praise be to the God and Father of our Lord Jesus Christ, the Father of compassion and the God of all comfort, who comforts us in all our troubles, so that we can comfort those in any trouble with the comfort we ourselves have received from God." Incredible nursing staff that is taking care of Terry. Placed order with Home Health for things we'll need.

June 11th — "Give thanks to the Lord for he is good; his love endures forever." I read the rest of Psalm 118 to Terry and we thanked God for taking care of us. He kissed my hands several times while I was reading aloud. It was one more awesome moment that we shared.

June 12th — Psalm 27:14 "Wait for the Lord; be strong and take heart and wait for the Lord." I'm going to talk to the team this Friday morning. It will be announced that Bill Lynch will take over for the '07 season.

June 13th — Isaiah 55:8-11 "'For my thoughts are not your thoughts, neither are your ways my ways,' declared the Lord. 'So is my word that goes out from my mouth; it will not return to me empty, but will accomplish what I desire and achieve the purpose for which I set it.'" Terry sat in a chair for two hours today! Drew came today with wonderful news. He got the job with US Airways Express and was able to tell his Dad. Special moment. Getting things ready to go home on Friday.

June 14th — No situation is hopeless for a believer – God is our hope and since He will never leave us or forsake us, we are always **HOPEFUL!** Amy and her boys will be here tomorrow. Football Youth Camp is Monday and Tuesday. Tucker, Spencer and Tate will attend. I had an unsettling experience tonight. While sitting on the bed beside Terry, I leaned over to say something to him. He immediately reached out and grabbed me around the neck and pulled me down. He did it in such a hard way that it almost hurt. And then he kissed my face. There was such urgency to that kiss and embrace. (Looking back I think this may have been his way of trying to say goodbye. Perhaps he had a glimpse of what was to come before I did.)

June 15th — Going home today! Wrote out all of Psalm 92. 7 a.m. meeting with the team. Joe (Palcic) picked me up — had a Starbucks for me. He was so thoughtful.

Going into Terry's office before I spoke was more emotional than I expected. The tears came without being invited the minute I stepped through the door. I wanted to be anywhere but where I was, doing anything except what I was about to do.

Here are the notes from my team talk:

From Coach Hep:

- Have a plan, work the plan, plan for the unexpected.
- Be in the right place at the right time.
- No problems, just opportunities.
- Trust — be committed to each other.

From Mrs. Hep:

- You and Coach are both on a mission.
- To reach your goals, you must do it a day at a time and not lose focus.
- Do it because it's right, not because it is easy.
- Sometimes we have to do it scared, but God will honor the effort.
- Look for opportunities to help someone else.
- We cannot be defeated, and we will not quit!

We left the hospital at 4:30 p.m. on that Friday afternoon looking forward to being home. The person in charge of our ambulance crew turned out to be a neighbor. He gave me his card and told me not to hesitate to call him if we needed help. He said his wife was also an EMT. The last thing I wanted to think about was needing an ambulance.

Allison and her family had left that day for Michigan to attend a wedding. It worked out well that Drew and Amy would be there to help with our arrival home. Our bedroom was on the second floor, so we decided it would be best to have Terry's bed in the family room. My kids insisted that I sleep in my bed which hopefully would provide a good night's rest. My nights in the hospital did not always prove restful.

Amy situated herself on one of the couches in the family room, grateful for the chance to be close to her dad. Drew set an alarm clock for every hour so that they could keep an eye on their father and make sure he was resting comfortably. Living in Ohio they were unable to be around as much as they wished and appreciated the opportunity to lend a hand.

At 4:15 a.m. on one of the hourly checks, they both realized that their dad was wide awake. In a voice that was surprisingly strong. He looked at them, and said, "I love you guys." He knew that they were taking care of him and those words spoke volumes to how he felt about his family.

The next day I had arranged for a woman to come to the house who could help me bathe him. As we stood on either side of him, I glanced down, and he was looking up at me. "I love you," he said. Bending over to kiss him, I said "I love you back." We finished the bath and made sure he was comfortable. Sometime that morning there was a knock at the door and in came Dave and Tammi, our EMT friends, bringing homemade BBQ and other goodies. It was such a thoughtful gesture and much appreciated.

While I was sorting medications and getting organized in general, Amy, Tucker and Spencer took advantage of the pool. The sound of the children playing was music to my ears. Drew said he would stay inside with his dad if I wanted to join them outside. It was an offer I couldn't refuse.

Amy and I were on the deck enjoying the sunshine when Drew came to the door and told me that he needed me to come inside. I heard a sense of urgency in his voice and when I stepped into the house he told me, "He's having trouble breathing. We need to do something."

Just like that our brief return home was about to come to an end.

6

He Left Us With a Smile

In less than 24 hours our time at home was over. Thankful that our EMT friend had left his card, Drew dialed the number and told him we needed help. His response was that he was on his way and Drew should hang up and call 911.

Dave and Tammi were at our house in a matter of minutes and began using the oxygen tank that they had brought with them. They worked feverishly until the ambulance arrived and transported Terry to Bloomington Hospital. Sitting in the front seat with the driver, I remember how surreal it felt to be retracing the route that had so recently brought us home. Another thought crossed my mind: Tomorrow, Sunday, June 17th, was Father's Day.

Amy and Drew took Tucker and Spencer to a family friend's house and then headed to the emergency room. At that point we were thinking that once they got his breathing problems under control, we would be able to take him home again.

We called Allison in Michigan, and she and her crew started for Bloomington. Anthony Thompson was also notified, and he joined us in the ER. The four of us waited for what seemed like an eternity until we were told that he was stabilized and would be going to the critical care unit. We went up to the floor where he was being moved and waited once again. After a while a doctor came out to see us. Drew remembers his exact words, "I feel that I need to emphasize the critical nature of this situation." The soberness of his caveat was not lost on us.

We continued our hallway vigil until we were at last allowed to go into his room. I just wanted him to know that we were there even though he couldn't respond to us. He was talked to, caressed, prayed over and kissed. We recognized and rested in the peace that saturated his critical care room. The nurses were so kind as they went about their work of monitoring and recording data. We would come and go, trying not to get in the way, but were content with holding his hand and standing close beside him.

Around 8 o'clock on that Saturday evening, we spoke with Dr. Larry Rink, and he assured us that they were doing everything they could, but it might be a good idea to call family. Larry was a friend of Terry's and an admirer of what he had accomplished during his brief tenure at IU. Undoubtedly, he had had this conversation with countless families, but his eyes revealed the sincerity of his sadness.

We phoned Terry's sister and brother, who in turn went to their mother's house to talk to her in person. Mark, Pam and her husband Jeff, and Phyllis were on their way to Bloomington as quickly as they could pack a bag. They arrived at the hospital around 1:30 a.m. and went right in to see Terry. My nephew, Paul, also came in the early morning hours and all of us spent the night going back and forth between the waiting room and Terry's side.

Daylight finally appeared and with it came the realization that it was Father's Day. It was the unspoken thought that I'm sure was on everyone's mind. Please don't let this special day be remembered as a sad one. Terry was stable, but there was no improvement. We had called Rick and Jenny Greenspan and the coaching staff too. They all arrived that afternoon.

Before they came another visitor had made his way to Bloomington to see Coach. Drew had called Ben Roethlisberger the night before and had been unable to reach him. He sent him a text, to which Ben immediately responded that he was in Los Angeles meeting with his agents. When he heard what Drew had to say, he began making arrangements to come to Indiana.

He wasn't able to get a commercial flight on such short notice, so he ended up chartering a plane to Bloomington. He called Drew on his way from the airport to find out where they would meet. They met at a side entrance and got to the elevator grateful that no one else was on it.

Just as the doors were about to close, a woman stepped in. She looked at Ben and said, "I know who you are! You're Ben Roethlisberger aren't you?" Ben kept looking straight ahead and replied, "No, I'm not. I just look like him." Drew said she was relentless in her demand to be answered. She was apparently miffed that he was preoccupied with a more pressing concern.

When I saw Ben, it was such a bittersweet feeling. I was so pleased for Terry that he had come, but I wanted to hear them talking about their latest round of golf or who their next opponent was. As difficult as it was, Ben rose to the occasion, and I know that whatever he said to Coach was understood and appreciated.

Before Ben left, our coaches had arrived. Ben was able to chat with some of these men who had been with him at Miami. Joe Palcic, Bobby Johnson, Brian George and Mike Yeager all played and/or coached in Oxford.

Linda and Bill Lynch brought trays of sandwiches and their thoughtful, practical gesture was very much appreciated. Rick and Jenny joined us, and I was reminded how all of these people had become like family. Curt and Jimmie Durnil made an appearance and it seemed right that they were there. A.T. and Lori, David and Bonnie Beecham continued to encourage us with their quiet strength.

We filled the waiting room and spilled out into the hall. Laughter could be heard, as well as hushed conversations and tears, but I felt surrounded by love and I know Terry did as well. By early evening our friends had gone home. Amy and Allison would eventually leave to be with their little guys and try to answer questions that I'm sure were troubling them. Drew and I spent another night in the waiting area. Actually, most of the hours passed sitting in chairs that had been placed beside Terry's bed. I talked to him, sang to him and whispered favorite verses that I knew he enjoyed hearing.

Monday brought an early morning visit from Joe Palcic who treated us with Starbuck's coffee and muffins. The three of us reminisced and talked about Coach. Joe had played for us when Terry was a defensive coordinator, and it was clear to us that someday he would join the coaching ranks.

On the bus coming home after away games, Joe would make his way to the front, find a spot close to Terry and proceed to pump him with questions about schemes, coverages and defenses. Joe would ask him about situations that had happened in the game, usually ending with, "What if?" He was a student of the game and reminded me of Terry when he was his age.

When Joe graduated, he and Coach had an understanding. When Terry got a head coaching job, Joe would be his first hire. He didn't have long to wait. The next year Terry was named Miami's head coach and arrived to find Joe waiting outside his office door at 6 a.m. on the morning the announcement was made. He wasn't taking any chances that Coach might have forgotten the deal they had made.

Monday was a quiet, waiting day that my kids and I shared with their dad. My sister was driving up from Alabama bringing my parents and brother, Paul. They got to the hospital at 10 p.m. and we all went in together to see Terry. We surrounded his bed and many prayers were lifted up on his behalf.

At about 12:30 a.m. everyone went home except Barb and Paul. Drew had gone to Wal-Mart earlier in the day and bought air mattresses to make resting a little more comfortable. I didn't spend much time on mine. It was hard to be away from him even though I was tired.

At about 4 a.m. I made my way back to him and stayed there. At 5 a.m. the nurse said that I should call my children. Everyone was staying at our house, and they knew when the phone rang what it meant.

Paul and Barb were with me until Amy, Allison and Drew came. We had become accustomed to watching the numbers on the monitors and understood what some of the more important ones meant. We noticed that the numbers were going down and suddenly people and equipment came flying into the room.

We were quickly ushered out and sobbed in disbelief that it had ended like this. To our surprise after about five minutes a nurse asked us back into the room. Dr. Rink said, "He's still with us, but only for a few more minutes. Now is your opportunity to say goodbye."

Upon entering the room I glanced out the window and saw the construction site where a building would one day stand. For the past several days we had watched bull dozers and other heavy equipment preparing the foundation for the new medical office. Now I was seeing the workers arriving for the day, lunch coolers in hand, greeting each other before beginning their day. There was such casualness in their demeanor that I couldn't understand. How could life be going on as usual when just across the street my world was being forever changed?

The chaos and noise of minutes before was gone. It had been replaced by a peace that we knew. Once more we surrounded him and each of our children had a chance to tell their dad what they wanted him to know.

My face was pressed against his as I whispered my last words to the love of my life. I didn't tell him goodbye, but instead "Watch for me because I'm coming, too."

As soon as his spirit left his body, the Terry Hoeppner I loved was gone. The part of him that made him who he was, was not his body but what was on the inside. We all had a sense of standing on sacred ground, and I wished I had been able to see the angels that I know were crowded into that room. His homecoming must have been something.

The nurse asked if she could remove some of the tubes and we huddled together with our arms around each other at the foot of his bed while she completed her task.

When she had finished, we turned back around and Amy gave out a gasp and said, "Look! It's his smile!"

And, sure enough, there was that half grin that we all knew. We stood there in awe of what God had just given us. For the four of us it was a confirmation that his pain was gone, and he was all right. One of Terry's favorite sayings was "Unexpected gifts at unexpected times."

I can't think of a better way to describe his gift of that smile.

7

Play 13

The 2007 football season is one that Indiana fans will never forget. Needless to say, I'm right there with them. It was an emotion-packed season for the players and coaches alike.

With pre-season camp starting only six weeks after Terry died, their focus was exactly where it needed to be. The players were steadfast in their goal to honor their former coach by "Playing 13." (12 regular season games plus a bowl game) Getting to a bowl game was one of Terry's goals when we arrived in Bloomington. Actually, the Rose Bowl was the one he mentioned in his first press conference and that aspiration never changed. "Strive for perfection, and settle for excellence" was how he described his work ethic. And he was relentless in challenging his guys to "Play 13."

Within a few days after Terry's death, a memorial service was being planned for the upcoming Saturday in Assembly Hall. I know there was so much time and effort that went into that endeavor. The IU staff responsible for the planning and execution (sounds like a football term!) went above all expectations. They paid attention to every detail, and we were very appreciative of their expertise.

By the service being in such a large venue, it afforded the opportunity for many to share in our tribute. When I look back on it, there is nothing I would change. Each person who spoke brought his or her own perspective of Coach and gave the attendees a very personal glimpse into what made him special.

When I told my children that I intended to say something, they all agreed to do the same. Once again, they had my back. When the service concluded, the team filed up to the front and each one offered his condolences and a hug. At the conclusion of the program people were directed to line the drive in front of Assembly Hall to pay their last respects. Seeing the team with helmets raised in a final salute was an image that will remain with me forever.

There was a brief graveside service and then we returned to the DeVault Alumni Center on campus for a gathering of family and friends. I was stunned by the number of colleagues and former players who had traveled to Bloomington. When you have coached as many teams as Terry had, it's easy to do the math. Hundreds and hundreds of lives had been impacted. Most of them, you hope, have been touched positively. From the turnout we saw, that must have been the case.

The next two months before the season began were challenging. The paperwork alone was a daunting task and I was grateful for the counsel of wise advisers and friends. It didn't help matters that I decided to put the house up for sale in September. Who puts a house on the market during football season? Surely not a coach's wife! I suppose I can plead temporary insanity and make a fairly strong case!

Game days were made even more interesting when out-of-town clients wanted to see the house. This happened several times and the routine was the same: hurrying home after the game, making sure everything was straight and then driving around town waiting until my realtor called telling me I could go home. I had invitations from people to stop by after the game, but I never felt comfortable doing it. I was trying to get used to the "new normal" that everyone talks about. Nothing about it felt normal.

Before each season begins, we had a tradition where the players were invited to their respective position coach's home for dinner and a time to enjoy each other away from the practice field and meeting rooms. That year I joined the fun at several of the cook-outs and loved hearing about what was happening with these young men whom I still thought of as Hep's guys.

Traditionally, the group that Terry took under his wing was the specialists: kickers, punters, holders and snappers. So I decided to have them to my house for dinner and a time of getting to know them better. It was an interesting mix of talent and high IQ's. The group included several doctors-to-be. They ate and swam and ate and played water volleyball and ate and entertained my grandkids and ate. You get the picture! It was so good to hear those sounds in my house again.

It was fun for me to hear their stories about Coach Hep and the banter that they had exchanged during warm-ups before practice. Austin Starr told me that he regretted not having achieved the level of camaraderie with Coach that the upperclassmen enjoyed. He had looked forward to the time when he could go into Coach's office, close the door and just talk.

I was able to get to know Kevin Trulock who, like Austin, was a kicker. I didn't realize that his dad had passed away from brain cancer as well. This had happened when Kevin was only 14 years old, one of three sons. I remember standing out by his car when they were leaving and letting him know how much admiration I had for him and his mother. Once again there was a sense of wonder at the friends God was putting in my path and a realization of how many hurting people there are.

The season opener was against Indiana State and our family was recognized on the field before the game. As we walked to midfield with President Michael McRobbie, the students began to chant Terry's name. As sad as I was, there was just as much gratitude. I was thankful that God had brought me to that moment.

I thought of Terry and what he was able to accomplish in such a short period of time. The most difficult part was the video presentation on the JumboTron scoreboard. It's one thing to see him, but it's another thing altogether to hear his voice. When we turned to leave the field, I saw the players in the end zone and could see how they had been affected as well. But I also saw how they responded. They got up and took care of business. The game of football lends itself to so many life lessons. And I was seeing one play out right before me.

Game days could have been a little awkward that first year because I wasn't sure where I would be sitting. The head coach's family suite is on the 7th level of the press box, and that's where we always sat. Linda Lynch graciously allowed us to use the box for one more season. She and Bill had two sons still playing college ball elsewhere and she wouldn't be at all of the IU games. I'm not sure I would have made it through that first season if my friend Linda hadn't come through for me. Our family had developed friendships with stadium staff and ticket takers. We especially enjoyed the scoreboard crew that worked in the box beside ours. It was energizing to see everyone and hear all of their Coach Hep stories.

During the walk, the coaches' families stand close to the stadium entrance to retrieve their children off of their daddy's shoulders and give good luck kisses to their husbands. When thinking about this scenario and how different it would be for me, I looked for a way to handle it positively. As I thought about the team and the expectations for it, I decided that I would write a note to the team captains and give it to them during the Walk. Captains Tracy Porter and Josiah Sears were leading the team and the plan was working as I had hoped. I handed each of them an envelope and got a hug in return. What happened next wasn't planned. Those two hugs turned into 100! The line was slowed down considerably, but it was worth the extra minutes it took. I was so proud of my Hoosiers!

After the Walk there was a two-hour period of time before kickoff. When Terry was coaching I would stay at the wives' tailgate and visit with family. After an hour or so I would go inside to his office and regroup. Closer to the start of the game, my kids would join me and we would make our way upstairs. It seemed strange knowing that my routine would not be that way again. About halfway through the season Terry Hutchens' book *Hep Remembered* came out. We did pregame book signings and it turned out to be enjoyable and therapeutic as well. Most people had some thought or story that they wanted to share and it was quite pleasant. Those two hours that I dreaded instead became time well-spent.

As for the season itself, everything that year built up to the Old Oaken Bucket game. When IU beat Ball State in a non-conference game the tenth week of the season, we became bowl eligible with six wins. But to really realize the goal to "Play 13" most people felt we needed to beat Purdue in the season ending match up at Memorial Stadium.

Early in Bucket week, I asked Bill if I could address the team. It was the first time I had spoken to them as a group since June. My heart was full of things that I wanted to tell them. While going through notebooks recently, I came across the speech I made to them on Tuesday, November 13th, 2007:

"First of all thank you for the opportunity to be a part of something great. This season may be a defining moment in many of your lives. I hope so. I love defining moments! They make us stronger. They help us see things a little clearer. They change **HOW** you think — before I was like this — **NOW** I'm like this.

That's how you grow.

Thank you for allowing me to stay connected with something I love. There's something reassuring to me about the sounds and sights, the smells and feel of the greatest game. Football has been such an important part of the love affair Coach and I shared for almost 40 years. I feel close to him when I'm with you.

There is no one in this room by accident. This team has been designed with each of you as a part. You have put yourself in this position by 6 a.m. winter workouts, spring practice, two-a-days, and weekly game preparation.

You HAVE what it takes!

You CAN do it!

My challenge to you is two-fold:

1) Make this week one where you do everything wholeheartedly, enthusiastically, without reservation. No effort will be half-hearted. Don't be double minded about any task, but embrace every drill, every sprint, every scouting report with all your heart and mind

and strength. I'm talking to each one of you — Pay attention to the details. Purpose in your heart and mind that before this week you never came close to how you're going to study and be ready. Do everything whole-heartedly!

2) Guard your hearts and minds. Don't let anything negative creep in. Let someone else read the blogs and newspapers. It doesn't make any difference what someone else thinks about you or this team. Talk is cheap – don't pay attention to it. Don't listen to anyone except your coaches, teammates and yourselves. Everyone else is an observer, a watcher — they don't have the investment you have. This will require self-control and motivation. No whining or complaining. No muttering under your breath or negative comments. Don't tolerate it from yourself or from your teammates. Guard you hearts and minds!

The victory is our,s and we will attain it TO-GETHER!

I love you all —
God bless —
GO HOOSIERS!"

Game time finally arrived and it appeared from the opening kickoff that everything was going our way. The first half seemed easy — maybe too easy — and we went into the second half hoping for a repeat of the first 30 minutes. For most of the first three quarters, we had it our way. We led 24-3 and the atmosphere was festive among Hoosier fans. I remember thinking this was going well, but I've been around this game long enough to not allow myself to feel overconfident.

At the end of the third quarter I realized why I was feeling that way. The momentum of the contest changed very quickly, and Purdue came back and tied it 24-all.

I was on the field at the beginning of the fourth period with Amy and Allison and their families. Drew had been unable to make the game and Amy was trying to give him a play by play on her cell phone. It was almost impossible to hear anything. But as crazy and hectic as it got in the last few minutes, I had a deep down sense that everything was going to be all right. I remember looking at the clock and thinking, "That's more than enough time to do what we need to do."

It couldn't have possibly been a more dramatic finish for an emotion-filled season. Hollywood could not have scripted it any better. Austin Starr, as it turned out, was the man of the hour.

As he stood there preparing for the kick, I was thrilled that he was the one who had the chance to seal the victory. I'll hear the voice of legendary IU play-by-play announcer Don Fischer making that call on the IU Radio Network forever. "The snap, the hold, the kick. IT'S GOOD! IT'S GOOD! AND THE HOOSIERS PLAY 13!!" Thank goodness for Youtube to be able to relive that moment anytime you like. It was quite a night.

When I think about the Bucket game, I can't help but think of something our friend Curt Durnil told us afterwards.

Curt and his parents stopped by the house after the game to join in the celebration. We were standing in the kitchen talking, but Curt stood close to the doorway. I heard his mother, Doretta, say to him, "Do you want to tell Jane what happened?" When I looked at him, I realized he had tears in his eyes. He was so emotional which is unlike the practical joker Curt that we knew. I couldn't imagine what in the world had happened.

He told me that he was standing on the sidelines at the end of the game with his stomach churning like everyone else's. He said he felt like after all they had been through, something was going to happen and Purdue was going to be able to sneak the game away from us. Then he said he looked to his right and he saw Coach Hep standing there looking out onto the field. He said he could see the left side of Coach's face, and he remembered the whole thing in remarkable detail. He said Coach had on his white IU hat and was wearing a red pullover.

He said he felt like Hep must have known what he was feeling because he lifted his right hand out of the fold it was in, grinned that Hep half-grin, pointed to the field and said, "Watch this."

We were stunned at hearing this, but when he said, 'Watch this' we lost it. That phrase means something special in our family. In 2003 at Miami we lost the first game, but went on to win the next 13 in a row.

Late in the season we trailed Kent State, and it was in the closing minutes of the game. The offense was getting ready to take the field and Coach was giving last second instructions. Right then Ben Roethlisberger walked across Terry's line of view to the field and said, "Watch this."

He then marched them down the field and scored to win the game. Terry loved to tell that story and that phrase became one of our family's favorites. And now for Curt to repeat those words made us all shake our heads and smile and cry. Curt still believes today that he saw what he saw and will never forget that moment he had with Coach Hep.

What a journey this season had been. I thought back to the first game and everything unknown that loomed ahead. Then I thought about hanging the 'I' on the Old Oaken Bucket in the locker room after that final game.

I thought about the fan base when we first got to Bloomington and then how they felt after Austin made that field goal. I thought about Terry's 84 speaking engagements during 2005 trying to spread the message that IU football was back. And then to be able to see what it meant on those faces after the game was very, very special.

We went on to play Oklahoma State in the Insight Bowl in Tempe, Ariz. It was IU's first bowl appearance since 1992. While it turned out to be a rather lopsided score against us, you can't discount what the team was able to accomplish. They succeeded against the odds, and it's a story they'll remember for the rest of their lives.

They "Played 13."

Jane, Terry and kids during days at Eastbrook, 1973.

WFL days while at preseason camp with Charlotte Hornets, 1974.

Terry with Drew in 1976.

Terry with kids and Coach Terrell Carter in Mullins, S.C., 1978.

Winkle enjoying life as The Queen.

Allison, Jane's mother Dorothy, Amy and Jane in Birmingham, 2008.

Terry and Quinn on The Walk, 2006.

Spencer with Anthony Thompson before Purdue game, 2007.

Terry displays the No. 20 Billy Cannon jersey, Christmas 2005.

Hoeppner family after the Coach Hep Cancer Challenge, 2009.

Christmas, 2004.

Terry with Quinn after the Independence Bowl, 2004.

Tate and Spencer at Terry's first spring game at IU, 2005.

At home with Ben Roethlisberger after the IU-Wisconsin game, 2006.

Terry and Jane, summer 2005.

Lake Monroe, summer 2005.

Joani Crean and Jane, summer 2009.

Eddie Getts, Jane and Marilyn Philpott, summer 2009.

At the airport after Miami-UCF game, Orlando 2003.

Singing the fight song at the 2003 Miami football banquet.

2003 GMAC Bowl trophy.

Terry and Drew at the Monroe (Ind.) County Airport, 2006.

Miami's football tribute to Terry and the retiring of Ben's jersey, 2007.

Jane and Terry's mother, Phyllis, at Hamilton Lake, summer 2009.

Hamilton Lake, summer 2009.

The last picture with Terry and his boys. 'V' is for Victory.

Putting the 'I' on the Old Oaken Bucket with Tracy Porter and Josiah Sears, 2007.

Steelers game, December 2007.

Franklin Homecoming, 1967.

Terry, with Tucker and Spence, after a hot spring practice at Miami, 1999.

Father's Day at the Red's game with four generations of Hoeppner men, 2000.

Jane and her sister, Barb, in Odessa, Ukraine, 2009.

An Elderly Home in the Ukraine, 2009.

William Rose

Following the Miami football awards banquet, December 2000.

Jane and her boys, Easter 2008.

Terry's induction into the Miami University Cradle of Coaches Association, 2008.

The family with Tammy and Jamie Walker at a Miami football game, 2008.

The boys at "The Rock," 2008.

On the field with Curt and Jimmie Durnil before Indiana State game, 2007.

Following one of Tucker's junior high football games, 2007.

The family in Tempe, Ariz. for the 2007 Insight Bowl.

The boys with Austin Starr at spring practice, 2008.

Spencer, Drew and Tate after running in the first Coach Hep Challenge, 2008.

Jane with Tracy, Josiah and their moms at The Walk, 2007.

The Madinger Family Reunion at Orange Beach, Alabama, 2009.

Terry with the MAC championship trophy, 2003.

Part Two

8

The Whisper

From the time that Terry passed away, there seemed to be opportunities for me to share our story. People were interested in knowing how God dealt with us during those 18 months.

The fact that I was able to speak of it, surprised me more than anyone. There are those who talk about being "called" and that brings to my mind a very clear, loud message. God has never treated me that way. He has been patient and gentle, sometimes nudging, but never harsh. I prefer to say that His leading is more of a whisper.

No one is exempt from troubles, and I continue to have challenges more often than I would like. It would be nice if circumstances always went according to our wishes, but I think it would make us very spoiled very quickly. God teaches us through adversity when we are focused on Him. The promise we have is that we don't need to go through trials alone. The 43rd chapter of Isaiah says it perfectly.

Fear not, for I have redeemed you;
I have summoned you by name;
You are mine.
When you pass through the waters,
I will be with you;
When you pass through the rivers,
They will not sweep over you.
When you walk through the fire,
You will not be burned.
And the flames will not set you ablaze.
For I am the Lord your God.

There are a multitude of lessons that my husband Terry and I learned during his 18-month battle with brain cancer. One of the most important for me was coming to appreciate the value of a new day.

Time is a gift that we can use or squander. We can't put it into a savings account and withdraw it when we need another hour in our day or add one more year to a good life. In my mind, I understood the importance of making each day count, but how could I consistently make that attitude a reality? I've often been guilty of having lofty intentions, but wasn't able to finish what I had set out to do. There had to be a way for me to "on purpose" treasure each day in the midst of difficulty and disappointment.

And so I very deliberately began the practice of starting my day with thanks to God for the gift of life and asking Him to let me be a blessing to someone. These petitions were lifted up before my feet hit the floor and any distractions began bombarding me. There was nothing flowery or lengthy about them — just straight to the point. Eventually, the morning ritual became a habit and it's one that continues today. This small act of dedication has helped me to recognize and acknowledge God's place in making the most of the time I've been given.

After Terry died it was hard for me to fathom what my life would be like without him. There wasn't a part of my soul that he hadn't touched, and I struggled as I thought of what was gone. But as everyone who has lost a loved one knows, you do what you have to do!

When I spoke at Terry's memorial service at Assembly Hall in June of 2007, it was basically to thank all of those who had loved and appreciated him. I also sensed that there might be something in what Terry and I had gone through that might encourage others. The fact that my children and I were able to address all of those gathered that day is a testimony to God's strength and grace. And for me it was the beginning of the path that my life would take.

Several weeks after the service, though not invited, the routine of the "new normal" had arrived. At about this same time came a request for me to speak at a women's gathering at Sherwood Oaks Christian Church in Bloomington. I agreed and began thinking about what I would say to the ladies. II Corinthians 1:4 tells us that "... we can comfort those in any trouble with the comfort we ourselves have received from God." Without a doubt, I knew what it was like to receive that encouragement.

And so two months after Terry's passing I'm standing in front of several hundred women telling our story. As I looked out over the audience, I saw Stacey Chupp. Stacey was a speech therapist at Bloomington Hospital, and she was crazy about Coach. She and Terry shared a love of NASA and the space program. I had never known anyone who could actually tell you where the space station was at any given moment! In a brief time Stacey had endeared herself to our family.

When I saw her in the audience it gave me a chance to thank her publicly for the care and love she had given to Terry and me. We had so many of those kinds of people in our life. Every one of them inspired us to keep the faith. When I finally got to my speech I was able to make it through without collapsing in a heap or running for the nearest exit! I took that as a sign of progress.

As I was heading down this uncharted road, my conversations with God usually included, "You have to make this clear to me! I have never done anything like this before. Lord, you are making the way for me and you're going to have to make it clear. Please put obstacles in my way if this isn't what you want me to be doing."

I found when I trusted God with my problems and decisions, He provided the peace. The Bible calls it the "peace that passes understanding." It can't be explained, only experienced. And it's not just there when all is going well. Interesting enough, it's even there when your heart is breaking.

I remember being at practice the fall after Terry died. I felt so much at home on the field and among all of those wonderful people who had been such an important part of our lives. But turning around to walk to my car by myself and having to drive home by myself, the tears would come. I just couldn't help it. But I found out that you can get through what you never thought you could. I remember Terry saying, "You may be scared, but do it scared." I think I've done that on occasions. I've done it scared, but I've done it.

The regularity of speaking requests was a surprise to me. I met so many people who had Coach Hep stories or had been through a situation similar to ours. They will never know the impact of their kind words on me.

I recently spoke to a group of high school freshmen. They are part of an initiative called 21st Century

Scholars. Each of them has an opportunity for a college scholarship if they are able to meet certain criteria. They must maintain a high grade point average, remain drug and alcohol free, and in general be a good citizen. These kids came from backgrounds where support was not the norm. What they were trying to accomplish would certainly require self-control and motivation.

Because this was a Bloomington-based group, they were familiar with Terry's mantra of "Don't Quit." It was definitely the message I wanted to convey. I told them that persevering had a two-fold effect. First of all, sticking to something helps keep you focused. They needed to understand that the things they were doing now would impact them later. Coach Hep called this W.I.N. — What's Important Now. It may be sitting in the front row in class or saying no to hanging out when you should be studying. Preparation **NOW** would result in achievement in the future. The second effect of having a will-not-quit attitude is that it is contagious. You are going to impact other people whether you know it or not.

I saw this first hand when we came to Indiana University. There were many who were incredulous that we would take a job that showed no promise. But for us the sky was the limit. This was an opportunity with **LIMITLESS** promise.

And so Terry set out about winning hearts and minds with his enthusiasm and love for this place. Was it always easy? No. But he wasn't looking for the easy way out. He wanted it done with integrity and knew the end product would be worth the hard work. Hopefully my high school friends in the 21st Century Scholars program were able to catch a glimpse of the vision I have for them. I picture them as successful achievers for whom perservering is a way of life.

Another one of my frequent questions in prayer,

when it comes to seeking purpose and focus in my life, is very simply the question, "What do you want me to do with my life?"

I can see people who are so good at presenting the gospel and others who are so good at teaching. I've always felt that the answer was that God wants me to encourage people.

One evening recently about the time I was having these thoughts and questions in my mind, I got a phone call from a woman who was in charge of a women's conference. She was calling to ask if I would speak, and I agreed to do that. As we were talking and firming up the details, I said to her, "Is there something specific you want me to talk about? Do you have something in mind or is there a theme that you're leaning toward?"

And she said, "No, we just want to be encouraged." I just had to smile. You've got to make it clear to me, God. And he just keeps doing that for me.

My recent life experience has given me a renewed sense of responsibility to reach out to others who are going through a rough time. Because I was on the receiving end of so many cards and well wishes, I never want to miss a chance to do the same for someone else. While my empathy level has definitely increased dramatically, there's a hesitancy on my part to initiate unsolicited advice.

An example of this occurred when someone in the community was going through what Terry had. A mutual friend suggested that I talk to the person or the parents or other family members. Because the idea had not come directly from the people involved, I declined. As it turned out they were not ready for that conversation, and I can completely understand their feelings. Maybe sometime in the future we'll have that talk, but it will be up to them.

There have been other instances of acquaintances

becoming close friends through the sharing of grief. Such was the case of my friend, Brenda.

Soon after our arrival at Indiana, a woman introduced herself to me during halftime of an IU basketball game. She told me that she had seen me at the hair salon and "just felt such a kinship with you." We chatted briefly and then returned to our seats. I saw her maybe once or twice in the next three years.

In December of 2008 I was invited to a charity auction by a friend. As we were discussing the event, she told me that we would be joined by a mutual friend who turned out to be Brenda. We looked forward to this time of becoming better acquainted, but that would come at a later date.

Brenda would not be coming after all because her husband Bob was having emergency surgery in Indianapolis. While attending a wedding in Arizona, he had been having headaches and was taken to the Mayo Clinic. He was diagnosed with a brain tumor and returned to Indiana. Bob passed away in February only three months after his surgery.

When I got the news it was all I could think about. My mind went back to the comment she had made about feeling a kinship with me. But this wasn't how I wanted us to become better acquainted! I wondered how would be the best way to get in touch with her and wasn't even sure that she was up to it.

On the following Saturday I had a rescheduled hair appointment. Because the shop was closed, my stylist Shanna and I were the only ones there. We were deep in conversation when we heard the sound of the front door opening. Shanna was explaining the situation when I heard a voice say, "I'm supposed to get my hair cut next week, but my husband's service is on Monday." She asked if Shanna could possibly help her out. Her daughter-in-law was with her and had insisted that she come.

I could tell Brenda was really struggling and close to tears, but she was doing one of those "just because you have to" things. When she came back to where I was, it was quite a moment. We exchanged hugs (with foil on my head and all!) and then Shanna worked her magic on my friend. Before she left we had a prayer together and I told her that things would not be the same, but she would be okay. "You feel broken and don't know how you'll go on, but you will," I told her. There was an unspoken bond between us that we would always share. And all of that happened because she reached out to me long before our husbands were ever sick.

Terry lived out his creed of never quitting. He used it with his football team and with his family. And when he fought and lost his battle with brain cancer in June of 2007, he maintained that very same attitude to the end.

Some people might look and say, "What good did it do? What good were the positive feelings and the feel-good message? In the end it didn't make any difference. He died anyway." To those people I say you missed the whole point. It's about the journey as well as the destination.

Another one of those lessons learned is that God has a plan for each of us. There's a reason I'm still here. God is teaching me about grace which is his unmerited favor. His favor cannot be bought or earned. I'm also learning that troubles are a guarantee in this world. But God will provide what we need to get through them and help us not to quit on the journey.

Before Terry was diagnosed in December of 2005, life couldn't have been much better for us. We had just finished our first season at Indiana University, and he was very quickly changing the football culture in

Bloomington. I was thrilled that he was able to coach at the university and in the state that he loved. But I was just as excited for the way Bloomington welcomed us and our family. I've said it before — they "got" him. They appreciated who he was and embraced his energy and enthusiasm. We were at home, and we knew it. There was absolutely no doubt that this was the place we were supposed to be. Because of that, there is so much irony in the way that it all worked out. Terry was having a once-in-a-lifetime experience, and he enjoyed every second of it. It was an amazing time for our family. To go from that high to the most difficult time in our lives, certainly the saddest, seemed impossible.

When I speak to groups, many things I relate have to do with my husband. Much of it has to do with the 18-month journey that we took together at the end of his life. I wouldn't trade those times we shared for anything.

The best thing about it is that we did it together, and we never, EVER, Quit!

9

"For Such a Time as This"

Everyone has heroes that they admire for how they behave under conditions that are less than ideal. It motivates us to see examples of people who are willing to take a stand even when there is a cost to their actions. We find strength in knowing that maybe we can muster up the same courage when we need it.

When my children were young and spent time with their grandparents in Birmingham, bedtime was a treat. My dad is a masterful storyteller and he thrilled Amy, Allison and Drew with the adventures of David and Goliath, or Joseph and his beautiful coat, or perhaps Joshua and the walls of Jericho. I must confess to standing outside the doorway and listening to the exciting stories of these heroes of the Bible. His words still ring in my ears, and I'm sure his colourful descriptions have remained in the minds of my children.

My favorite hero is Esther. Maybe I could relate to her because she was a woman, but whatever the reason she was the one that captured my mind and heart. Here is the story of a young Jewish girl who was orphaned and adopted by her older cousin, Mordecai.

She was a beauty described as "lovely in form and feature." Because of her appearance, she was selected to be part of King Xerxes' household and was shown favor there. Mordecai would daily come to the courtyard walls and check on her welfare.

Esther had not revealed her background to anyone, but that was about to change. Among the intrigue there was a plot against Mordecai and a decree to put to death all of the Jewish people. Mordecai pleaded with Esther to ask the king for mercy on behalf of her people.

The law at that time said anyone who approached the king without being summoned would be put to death. The only exception was for the king to extend his gold sceptre and thus spare the person's life.

Mordecai's message to Esther ended with the haunting words, "And who knows but that you have come to royal position for such a time as this?" To this Esther replied that Mordecai and all the Jews should fast for three days, just as she and her maids would be doing. At the end of that time she would approach King Xerxes with her request, and she added, "I will go to the king even though it is against the law. And if I perish, I perish."

Now, that's commitment!

The king granted her petition, and her life was spared. There were several more twists and turns, but Esther's bravery and boldness saved her people. Because of her willingness to go the distance regardless of the outcome, she was indeed the one "for such a time as this."

Whoever your heroes are, they undoubtedly have helped you by example to be a little braver and stronger.

When faced with difficult times, it's easy to give up. Or to rephrase that statement, when faced with difficult times, it's hard to keep going. It's true either way you say it.

Sometimes it feels like the deck is stacked against you and your back can't be any closer to the wall. It's just for these times that we need to be armed to fight the good fight.

Jesus said in Matthew 4:4 that we don't live by bread alone, "but by every word that proceeds out of the mouth of God." That tells me that there is a part of me that needs to be fed and nourished that is not related to my physical body. I understand the importance of regular, well-balanced meals and how they give me strength and energy. I also realize what would happen if I decided to stop eating. The parallels between our physical and spiritual natures enable us to understand how imperative it is to keep them both healthy.

Being spiritually fit requires regular time spent in reading God's Word and praying. This has been a battle for me because there is always the excuse of being too busy or just not feeling like doing it. But as is the case with any beneficial exercise, we must apply ourselves with effort and a determination of doing the task at hand. Our spirit is willing, but our flesh is weak. While this may be true, we can't use it as an excuse for avoiding what we know is best for us.

Obviously, there are days when my quiet time is longer than others, but I try not to miss it altogether. And like developing any habit, it will eventually become a part of your daily routine. When talking about this with others, they are sometimes at a loss at where to begin.

The book of Proverbs lends itself to a user-friendly devotional plan. Because if contains 31 chapters, each one can correspond to a day of the month. If it's the 15th day, I'll read the 15th chapter and so on. If you miss a day, it's simple to get back on track. The important thing is you are seeking God, and when you do that, you will find Him.

You may find that placing verses around your house in strategic places can be very helpful. During our last 18 months together I had "reminders" on our bathroom mirror and above the kitchen sink. The scripture on the mirror was written on a post-it note by our daughter Amy. I still have it and remember how it gave us encouragement. Joshua 1:9, "Have I not commanded you to be strong and courageous? Do not be terrified. Do not be discouraged. For the Lord your God will be with you wherever you go."

We read that every day. Lana, our friend who helps with cleaning the house, told me later that she was always careful when she sprayed our mirror. She didn't want the Windex to touch the note. She also had to work around the one that was taped to a shelf over the kitchen sink. It was a passage from Ephesians that Josiah Sears' mother had sent us. I saved that reminder as well.

On many occasions people have said to me, "You are so strong!" And I say, "Clearly, you don't know me!" God gets all the credit for giving me the "want to" and the strength to keep going. I found myself always using Terry's motto of 'Don't Quit' when speaking to various groups. I could go on at length about his philosophy of perseverance and the role it played in our life.

One day I decided to see what the Bible has to say about maintaining an attitude of not giving up. There were many verses that provided muscle to strengthen and feed my spirit. It's my hope that by sharing them perhaps you feel that same comfort that the word of God can provide.

Hebrews 10:23,24 "Let us hold unswervingly to the hope we profess, for he who promised is faithful. And let us consider how we may spur one another on to love and good deeds." This tells me that first of all we must hang in there and not let go. I love the word unswervingly — it perfectly describes having strong determination. Secondly, it says we should impact others in such a way that they will love and do good deeds. This cuts to the chase about how we should live our lives. We are not victims, but instead have life with purpose. Lastly, we are reminded that God is faithful. He keeps his promises.

James 1:12 "Blessed is the one who perseveres under trial, for when he has stood the test he will receive the crown of life that God has promised to those who love Him." This verse is underlined in my Bible and dated 1/3/07. It was Spencer's memory verse for that week, and Terry and I learned it along with him. It provides such incredible words of encouragement and hope.

Hebrews 10:35 "So do not throw away your confidence; it will be richly rewarded. You need to persevere so that when you have done the will of God you will receive what He has promised." Once again this verse is underlined and dated 10/1/06. We must have needed this "food" for whatever was going on for us right then.

Each of these scriptures refers to a reward to be received. There is an emphasis on what we do in the present impacting us in the future. This can't be talking about material possessions that surround us here. We can't take any of that with us when we die. They will all eventually belong to someone else.

Matthew 6:19-21 "Do not store up for yourselves treasures on earth where moth and rust can destroy and thieves can break in and steal. But store up for yourself treasures in heaven where moth and rust cannot destroy. And where thieves cannot break in or steal. For where your treasure is, there your heart will be also." This is a reminder to me to keep my priorities straight and to put my trust in God and not in things. It gives me such joy to know that Terry trusted in his Heavenly Father also. My "treasure" went to heaven on the 19th of June, 2007.

Being strong and refusing to quit does not come without times of doubt and fear. But I've always believed strongly that the more we trust the less room there is for fear.

I John 4:18 "There is no fear in love. Perfect love casts out fear." I'm always looking for practical ways to grow in my faith. One method I have learned that works for me is to speak the Word out loud. This may sound bizarre, but it works. And because I live by myself, there is no chance of bothering anyone else! When I'm trying to learn anything by heart it always helps to repeat it aloud. When I say a verse over and over, there is sometimes an understanding that comes with the repetition. I may think about it in a way that I never had before. This is a way that I hide God's Word in my heart, so that it's there when I need it.

One passage I say on a regular basis is **Psalm 121**. I love how it begins. "I lift my eyes to the hills. Where does my help come from?" Aren't there times when you are just waiting for the cavalry to come riding in and rescue you?

As a warrior, David understood the importance of reinforcements and getting help when you need it. But more than that, he placed his trust in something more than horses and artillery. "My help comes from the Lord, the maker of heaven and earth."

I like to change the *your* to *my* and the *you* to *me* when reading the Psalms. It makes it very personal. "He will not let my foot slip. He who watches over me will not slumber. Indeed, He who watches over Israel will neither slumber nor sleep. The Lord will watch over my life. He will be the shade at my right hand. The sun will not harm me by day nor the moon by night. The Lord will keep me from all harm. He will watch over my life. The Lord will watch over my coming and going both now and forevermore."

When I examine this passage, it covers everything I need. Number one, I know His eyes are on me all the time and He's not asleep at the switch. He cares for me and wants to keep me from harm. He's my protector. He knows my comings and goings. And He's doing this for me right now and forever. Wow, it doesn't get any better than that!

The Bible says that God inhabits the praises of his people. When we lift our voices, the promise is that He is there. When we are in a corporate worship setting, the sense of God's presence is real. I found praise music to be especially helpful in the months following Terry's passing. I listened to the MercyMe CD, *Coming Up To Breathe*, so many times that I'm surprised it didn't fall apart! I listened almost exclusively to two tracks that captured where I was at that time.

I gave a copy to a friend assuring her that No. 3 and No. 8 were the best songs on the disc. I knew all of the words, but wasn't sure about the titles! Music was very instrumental (no pun intended) in helping my heart heal and experience God's peace. The first of those songs is called, "Hold Fast." Read the lyrics, and I think you'll understand exactly what I mean.

"Hold Fast"

By MercyMe

To everyone who's hurting
To those who've had enough
To all the undeserving
That should cover all of us
Please do not let go
I promise there is hope

Refrain
Hold fast
Help is on the way
Hold fast
He's come to save the day
What I've learned in my life
One thing greater than my strife
Is His grasp
So hold fast

Will this season ever pass?
Can we stop this ride?
Will we see the sun at last?
Or could this be our lot in life?
Please do not let go
I promise you there's hope

(Refrain)

You may think you're all alone
And there's no way that anyone could know

What you're going through
But if you only hear one thing
Just understand that we are all the same
Searching for the truth
The truth of what we're soon to face
Unless someone comes to take our place
Is there anyone?
All we want is to be free
Free from our captivity Lord
Here He comes

(Refrain)

If there was ever a song written just for me, it would be "Hold Fast." It gave me hope when I had white knuckles and thought I would surely fall. There were times when I felt alone and knew that no one else could possibly imagine what I was going through. But God's grasp and grace **WERE** greater than my strife. I would listen to those words, and it would give me the strength to hang on and know that it would be all right.

The second MercyMe song that really speaks to me is track No. 8 off that same CD, *Coming Up To Breathe*. The title of the second song is "Bring The Rain." Again, it is my hope by printing these lyrics that you will find strength in the awesome power of God.

"Bring the Rain"
By MercyMe
All Rights Reserved. Used By Permission.

I can count a million times
People asking me how I
Can praise you with all that I've gone through
The question just amazes me

Can circumstances possibly
Change who I forever am in You

Maybe since my life was changed
Long before these rainy days
It's never really ever crossed my mind
To turn my back on you, Oh Lord
My only shelter from the storm
But instead I draw closer through these times
So I pray

Refrain
Bring me joy, bring me peace
Bring the chance to be free
Bring me anything that brings you glory
And I know there'll be days
When this life brings me pain
But if that's what it takes to praise you
Jesus, bring the rain

I am yours regardless of
The dark clouds that may loom above
Because you are much greater than my pain
You who made a way for me
By suffering your destiny
So tell me, what's a little rain?
So I pray

(Refrain)

Holy, holy, holy
Is the Lord God Almighty

There were many times that I would wake in the
night and "Hold Fast" or "Send The Rain" would be
going through my mind. Even when I was sleeping that

music was ministering to me. There was one other song, "Voice of Truth" by Casting Crowns, that spoke to me in the same way. I'd like to share the lyrics to that song as well.

"Voice of Truth"
By Mark Hall and Steven Curtis Chapman

Oh what I would do to have
The kind of faith it takes to climb
out of this boat I'm in
Onto the crashing waves

To step out of my comfort zone
To the realm of the unknown where Jesus is
And he's holding out his hand

But the waves are calling out my name
and they laugh at me
Reminding me of all the times
I've tried before and failed
The waves they keep on telling me
Time and time again, 'Boy, you'll never win!'
'You'll never win.'

But the voice of truth tells me a different story
And the voice of truth says, 'Do not be afraid!'
And the voice of truth says, 'This is for My glory'
Out of all the voices calling out to me
I will choose to listen and believe the voice of truth.

Oh what I would do to have
The kind of strength it takes to stand before a giant

With just a sling and a stone
Surrounded by the sound of a thousand warriors
Shaking in their armor
Wishing they'd have had the strength to stand

But the giant's calling out my name
and he laughs at me
Reminding me of all the times
I've tried before and failed
The giant keeps on telling me
Time and time again, 'Boy you'll never win!'
'You'll never win.'

But the stone was just the right size
To put the giant on the ground
And the waves they don't seem so high
From on top of them looking down
I will soar with the wings of eagles
When I stop and listen to the sound of Jesus
Singing over me

I will choose to listen and believe the voice of truth.

I've always found strength in music and those three songs are wonderful examples of the way God can speak to us in that way. I do choose to listen and believe the voice of truth.

There's no doubt that in dealing with the death of a spouse or a loved one or in providing care for someone during a difficult time, that you are constantly looking for strength. But maybe you are reading this and haven't experienced any of those situations yet.

Hopefully, you will be able to relate to what I call the ultimate "Don't Quit" experience. Marriage. It requires effort and determination and creativity. Terry and I found out how strong the bond of marriage is. It didn't happen overnight and it wasn't easy. There were times of doubt and wanting our own way. But we refused to give up on what we had committed to and started putting each other's needs above our own. We learned to accept each other and not try to make each other into something we weren't. We remained boyfriend and girlfriend through it all.

A few thoughts about marriage:
- It is better at the end than it was at the beginning.
- When you get over yourself, the fun really starts.
- Your heart can skip a beat when you're 50 and older!
- You can be best friends.
- There's something to be said about a companionable silence.
- Recognize your differences.
- Cherish your shared principles.
- Never forget the value of your treasure.

I was married for 39 years to the love of my life. You may have only begun the journey or are somewhere in between. In whatever season you find yourself, know that it is worth the effort in the end.

10

It's Going to Be Okay

There are few words to describe the feeling of losing your soul mate. There is an unfamiliarity about it that is a constant reminder of what has been lost. Many of you know exactly what I mean because you are also members of a club that you didn't want to join.

I found that the clichés that I had heard all of my life were for the most part true. Everyone except you does go back to their routine and picks up where they left off. And this must happen because there are children and jobs and responsibilities to take care of. The phone calls and visits did slow down, but they came when I needed them.

I found that the simple pleasures were the ones I missed the most. I can't imagine how many times I placed two coffee cups by the pot waiting to be filled, both with cream and a little sugar added to one. Old habits are hard to break, but the day did come when I smiled rather than cried at the sight of his cup.

Learning to eat alone was another hurdle that I didn't very much appreciate. Most of my meals I ate standing at the kitchen counter while assuring myself that cereal is one of the food groups! For all intents and purposes I operated between the kitchen, study, laundry room and bedroom. I avoided the family room because of how much time Terry and I had spent in it. It was easier not to go there. I could read or watch television elsewhere, except that reading for pleasure was impossible for me to do. I wondered if I would ever read a novel again and at that point didn't care one way or the other. Trying to stay with the storyline about fictional characters was asking too much.

My Bible was the only book that kept my attention. I received many books about being a widow, but it would be months before I opened any of them. It was the same with crossword puzzles or word games that I had always found enjoyable. I knew that the day would come when I would revisit these pastimes, but I wondered how long it would take for that desire to come back.

Thankfully, one challenge had been resolved on the morning of June 19th, and it felt good to know I could check it off of the list of 'firsts.' When Amy, Allison, Drew and I came home from the hospital, we knew the first order of business had to be talking to the little guys about what had happened.

All of us including their dads, Steve and Drew, gathered in the family room. I tried to explain that Pa would not be coming home, but that we would be together again in heaven. It was little comfort to them when they wanted him right now and couldn't believe that what I was saying was true. I asked them each to tell what they liked best about Pa and it was no surprise to find that he was their best playmate.

As Tate told me on the way to the cemetery, "It's

just no fun without Pa." Through tears and laughter we continued to talk about him and reassure them of his love for each of his boys. It was an emotionally charged as well as draining conversation for all of us, and when it concluded I went upstairs to rest. I collapsed on his side of the bed because I wanted to feel close to him and cried myself to sleep.

When I woke up from that nap, I knew that I would never again lie on my side of the bed. It was a small victory, but one for which I was grateful. I realized later what a good choice this had been.

Over a year later Tate was spending the night and I was tucking him into 'my side' of the king-sized bed. He asked me to read him a story and I crawled in beside him, loving that special closeness that comes at bedtime. But I felt something else as well when I looked at the empty spot on the other side of the bed. I missed Terry! The bed hadn't seemed empty when I was on his side. On the contrary, it had provided a sense of comfort that became my 'normal.'

I found that knowing the 'right' time to do things was tricky. There are lots of opinions about when to get rid of your spouse's belongings, and I didn't really pay attention to any of them. I let my children choose anything they wanted and gave other family members things that I thought they might like to have. But much of it stayed in the closet which became a place where I could go and have a good cry. After I would have my moment of tears, I felt better and returned to whatever I had been doing. The frequency of the "closet visits" lessened, and I began to find that as time passed my heart was on the mend slowly but surely.

As I went about all of those dreaded tasks that had to be completed, every now and then I would receive one those God-hugs. One happened to me at the Bureau of Motor Vehicles of all places. Our car had been in both of our names, and I needed to have it changed to only mine. As I waited in the famous BMV line, I wanted to be anywhere but where I was standing at that moment. Fighting tears and the urge to bolt, I looked across the crowded room and saw Greg Brown. Greg was one of our defensive linemen, and I can't tell you how good it felt to see a familiar face. He gave me a big bear hug and will never know how much I needed his encouragement at that second.

As a coach's wife I was used to being on my own during two-a-days in preseason camp. This was a time when you didn't have to worry about your husband and most wives looked forward to the flexibility of meal planning and enjoying the end of summer vacation.

Even though he was not a part of the daily schedule for a while, we managed to grab a bite together occasionally and would visit briefly about what was happening with our kids and grandkids. Those several weeks would pass quickly, and we would once again be into the routine of the season. It was becoming obvious to me now, how much time and effort I had spent planning things around him.

I'd like to think that I wasn't distracted during this time, but something happened that made me change my mind. I got the opportunity to meet two more wonderful people, Jim and Joanne, but unfortunately we got acquainted while they repaired my garage door. Not once, but twice, I had backed into it while trying to exit my garage. I'm not sure what I did, but I was so aggravated with myself for being careless ... TWICE!

Someone gave me Jim's name and said he was the best. When his white truck pulled in my driveway I was surprised to see that he had his wife with him. They were quite a team, and I appreciated their devotion to each other as well as their expertise.

They tried to comfort me by telling a story about a

woman who had driven her car forward through the garage wall and into her bedroom! They didn't want me to be too hard on myself and thought it would be helpful for me to know that it could be worse. Jim and Joanne did turn out to be the best at their trade, but they were also the perfect encouragers for someone who was having a very difficult day.

While there were brand new challenges for me to face as I tackled life by myself, there were areas about which I felt competent. Terry had always handled our finances, and it was not anything that was up for discussion. That was his responsibility, and I was good with the way it was. But when I stopped teaching and had more time on my hands, it was a job that I insisted he relinquish to me. His hours were long enough without having to be concerned about paying bills.

When we made the move to Bloomington from Oxford, I did all of the house selling and buying duties. I was so grateful that this was not something I was going into blindly. I've heard of women not knowing the first thing about a budget and I thought how that described me for many years.

There were "gotchas" that happened without warning, and there was nothing I could do to prepare myself for their sudden attacks. When I opened a new box of checks, I stared in disbelief at seeing only my name on the front. PGA (golf) publications kept arriving for him, and I would melt when I saw them. A bottle of merthiolate brought me to tears because it was his cure-all for everything. My children can attest to his fact because they all remember having orange knees and elbows where dad had applied his wonder drug. My job was to blow on the wounded area so it wouldn't sting so much. Being able to laugh with my family about some of these painful memories has been helpful for us all.

My house had been on the market from September

'07 to February '08 without any serious offers. I met with my realtor, who had become my friend and confidante, about how to proceed. She suggested looking at different ways to market it, but I felt that if it was supposed to sell at that time, it would have. I made the decision to 'burn my boat' which in our family is a phrase that means to step out into the deep and trust God. I decided to take it off the market and wait for a while. My thinking about the house was the same thinking I had about Austin's game-winning field goal against Purdue in 2007. I had every confidence that he would make the kick, and I had faith that my house would sell.

In the interim I stayed busy with speaking engagements and preparing for the Bible study that I taught every Friday morning at Sherwood Oaks. I was motivated by all of the young women who were making time in their busy schedules to grow in their faith walk. I was making progress as well and knew that God was providing what I needed when I needed it.

I was also busy with the planning of a project that had been in the works since the previous fall. Dr. Rick Schilling had approached me in August about the possibility of starting an annual fundraising event for cancer research in Indiana. He had never met Terry, but was moved by his story and wanted to do something in his name. He had lost his father-in-law and best friend to cancer and felt compelled to do something. I was amenable to the idea, but not ever having done anything of this nature, I was probably not very helpful.

Jennifer Hurtibise, Steve Mangan, Rick and I were the core group and we eventually added more members who provided expertise in a variety of areas. We plowed ahead making plans for the first annual Coach Hep Indiana Cancer Challenge. It was held on May 10th and successfully attracted over 700 runners, walkers and bikers.

That May I attended the graduation ceremony at Franklin College. The previous year they had awarded an honorary degree to Terry, but he was unable to accept it. It was decided that it would be bestowed posthumously, and I accepted in on behalf of my family. I had been to Franklin earlier in the spring for a Phi Delta Theta dinner where they announced the first recipient of the Terry Hoeppner Scholarship. Walking through campus it was impossible not to think back 40 years and wonder where the time had gone.

Reality brought me back to Bloomington and a summer of activities for which I was grateful. I looked at my calendar and was amazed to see how full it was. I couldn't help noticing that June 19th was not far away and would mark the most poignant of all the 'firsts.' As with every other hurdle that I faced, God provided a way for me to get over it.

This day of such significance for our family would be spent in Shreveport, Louisiana. I had gotten a call several months earlier from a representative of the Independence Bowl asking if I would be willing to attend their Hall of Fame induction. They would be honoring Terry and Nick Saban as coaches who had distinguished themselves during their Independence Bowl appearances.

I immediately agreed to come and asked the date of the ceremony. She replied, "June 19th." Wow! When I hung up the phone all I could think was, "Thank you Lord. I can't think of a better thing to do on that day!" I was thrilled that Amy and Allison could accompany me and knew that we would make it through. Accepting that honor made the anticipation and reality of that day, one of gratefulness and excitement with a little sadness, rather than the other way around.

In July I called my realtor with my decision to put the house back on the market. The first showing was to people who were interested, but were going on vacation and didn't want to do anything until they got back. The second people who went through it bought it! I immediately began a search for a new place that would be the perfect fit for what I needed. I also began the task of sorting through memorabilia and keepsakes making choices about what to keep and what to part with.

Another important decision had to be made and that was what to do with Winkle. She had remained an outdoor cat, but was much loved by all of us, especially the little guys. There were loud cheers when I told them the news that Winkle would join me inside my new house. There were also incredulous looks when I showed them what I had found while sorting through old jewelry.

Years ago I received a 'cat pin' as a birthday gift from a teacher friend. I laughed and told her that we preferred dogs and not cats, but I would wear it because she had given it to me. It had long since faded from my memory and had stayed in the box with the other 'teacher jewelry.' I caught my breath when I saw it. It was a perfect gray and white replica of Winkle! It looked as though Winkle had been hand-picked just for me.

Family and friends were concerned that I would be sad leaving the home that Terry and I had shared. Yes, there would be sadness, but there would also be excitement and anticipation of what was ahead for me. God was making a way for me and reminding me daily that everything would be okay.

11

Living Life on Purpose

One thought that is constantly on my heart is the idea of living life on purpose. To me, it's more than just a catchy phrase. It's truly a way of life.

I did a Bible study about living life with purpose, and that class was taught during the time that I was preparing to move to my new house. I can still see myself typing on a little table where the desk had been before I sold it. I was surrounded with packing boxes and the last minute clutter that comes with moving. When I look at the material, it reveals what God had placed on my heart at that time. It is my hope that there may be something in it that speaks to you as well.

I debated on whether I should change the words to make it more in book form or if I should just leave it exactly how I used it during the three weeks we completed this study. I decided I liked it just the way it was and would make it Chapter 11 of this book. Again, I hope God can speak to you through the words of this study.

Introduction

My purpose in planning this Bible study is to encourage you ladies to become actively engaged in your faith-walk. God is showing me how to seek him daily in all situations. Because we are at different places in our spiritual lives, it's going to be fun to see how God reveals himself to each of us. God knows each of you here intimately, and there is no one present by accident. May I say that each of you is here **ON PURPOSE!**

As we spend the next three weeks together, we're going to be looking at how the Bible says we are to live. We all bring baggage and history with us, but our need for God is the same. Some of you may be at a time of grieving and sorrow right now. Others may be experiencing a fairly smooth ride for the time being. The point is that we desperately need God regardless of our circumstances, and God is able to meet us wherever we are. Paul was able to say, "… for I have learned to be content whatever the circumstances." The impact of this verse for me has always been that Paul said it while being beaten and chained. But as I studied it, I began to see that Paul said he learned to be content. No magic wand or secret potion. He learned to apply the Word to each and every situation in which he found himself.

So, girlfriends, we're going to **LEARN** how we can live according to God's word and not be pushed around by all of the world's quick fixes and fancy remedies. I want us to be grounded in something that cannot be shaken, regardless of what the world throws at us.

Proverbs 4:23-27 "Above all else, guard your heart, for out of it is the wellspring of life. Put away perversity from your mouth; keep corrupt talk from your lips. Let your eyes look straight ahead, fix your gaze directly before you. Make level paths for your feet and take only ways that are firm. Do not swerve to the left or to the right, keep your feet from evil."

This verse speaks so clearly to my heart about how much I am involved in choosing to live life on purpose. I must be the one who guards my heart by not talking perversely or corruptly. That obviously requires self-control. No one except **ME** can decide what will come out of my mouth or **NOT** come out of my mouth.

Today we're going to examine the Word and see what God says about how to keep our lips and eyes and feet where they need to be. And how to keep on a path that is straight and not swerving all over the place!

We will look at three areas that impact a believer's walk.

1. ATTITUDE (not a new concept for a coach's wife).

While it is true that we are sometimes not in control of circumstances that somehow find us, we are nonetheless in charge of how we respond or react. Of course, the story of Joseph comes to mind as an example of circumstances versus attitude.

We all know the story of the favorite son with the beautiful coat and his jealous brothers. When Joseph told them about the dream of his sheaf of grain standing up and theirs bowing down to it, his brothers began to plot to kill him. Instead of murdering Joseph, he was sold into slavery for 20 pieces of silver. His brothers dipped the robe into the blood of a goat and told their father that Joseph must have been killed by a wild animal. While his father was mourning his death, Joseph was in fact bought by Potiphar, one of Pharaoh's officials. Joseph was 17 years old.

Genesis 39:2,3 says, "The Lord was with Joseph and he prospered." (He had gone through a horrific experience and now it looked as though things were looking up! I added that!) "When his master saw that the

Lord was with him and that the Lord gave him success in everything he did, Joseph found favor in his eyes and became his attendant."

The blessing was so strong on Potiphar's house that he put Joseph in charge of everything except his wife and the food he ate. Potiphar's wife had taken notice of Joseph and implored him to sleep with her. He refused and tried to explain that her husband had entrusted him with everything except his wife. He would not "do such a wicked thing and sin against God." Sometime later he was alone with her and she begged him again, but he ran from the house leaving his cloak behind. When Potiphar returned home, his wife said Joseph had accosted her and would only leave after she screamed for help.

So Joseph was put back in prison not because of something he had done, but because of a lie. Once again God was with Joseph, and he was shown kindness and favor. I marvel at the attitude that Joseph was able to maintain. He was able to correctly interpret dreams of his fellow prisoners the cupbearer and the baker. He asked the cupbearer to remember him to Pharaoh when he was restored to his position, but it was not to be. The cupbearer forgot Joseph, and he would remain in prison for two more years.

At the end of this time Pharaoh was having disturbing dreams and the cupbearer at last remembered the young Hebrew man who interpreted dreams. And so Joseph's time with Pharaoh began and would evolve into being in charge of the entire nation's food supply. He was second in command and respected by all. Pharaoh said, "Can we find anyone like this man, one in whom is the spirit of God?" Joseph kept a heart for God, and everyone knew it.

The story of course ends with his brothers coming for food because of a drought and Joseph recognizing them even though they didn't know him. After several trips to Egypt following the orders of Joseph, they are finally united. When his identity is made known, he tells his brothers, "Do not be distressed and do not be angry with yourselves for selling me here, because it was to save lives that God sent me ahead of you."

Joseph served God with his whole heart. His motive was to please God in whatever circumstances he found himself. He served others in the palace and in jail in a godly way — while in despair at being alone and forgotten. He walked in love when he had every reason to be bitter. And because he maintained an attitude of dependence on God, he was used in a mighty way.

I want to develop an outlook that is based on more than feelings. To entrust my heart to how I 'feel' about something is a recipe for disaster. Feelings are based on emotions and while some emotions may be enjoyable, others can be destructive and hurtful. They are certainly not trustworthy. Joseph's story would have quite a different ending if he had based his reactions on feelings.

As a believer my attitude is rooted in who God says I am and the future I have in Him. **Psalm 16:5,6** says, "Lord you have assigned me my portion and my cup; you have made my lot secure. The boundary lines have fallen for me in pleasant places; surely I have a delightful inheritance."

As a believer my attitude should not be based on anything the world has to offer.

Proverbs 23:17,18 "Do not let your heart envy sinners, but always be zealous for the fear of the Lord. There is surely a future hope for you and your hope will not be cut off." God is cautioning us to guard our hearts against envying the 'stuff' of the world. He says instead of being preoccupied in what someone else has, to use that energy to seek him zealously. If we lose the zeal, we lose the reverential awe of who God is.'

I John 2:15-17 "Do not love the world or anything in the world. If anyone loves the world, the love of the Father is not in him. For everything in the world – the cravings of sinful man, the lust of his eyes and the boasting of what he has and does — comes not from the Father, but from the world. The world and its desires pass away, but the one who does the will of God lives forever."

It doesn't take too many hours without electricity to see how dependent we are on TV and the computer. They occupy much of my time and energy. I'm sure we all have made attitude adjustments while waiting for the power to come back on!

2. MOTIVE

The Bible has much to say about what kind of motives are pleasing to God. He is not a big fan of the ends justifying the means. If we choose to do the right thing with the right heart, God will take care of the ending.

Proverbs 16:2 "All a man's ways seem pleasing to him, but motives are weighed by the Lord."

How many times do we do something with the motive of appearances rather than letting God bless someone through us? Do we give gifts with no strings attached or with the expectation of receiving something in return? Do we keep track of who thanked us and who didn't? Ouch!

I Corinthians 4:5 "He will bring light to what is hidden in darkness and will expose the motives of men's hearts. At that time each will receive his praise from God."

We will receive praise from God for having pure motives. This encourages me to guard my motives with a pure heart because I know that nothing is hidden from

God's eyes, and I want what is not seen to be pleasing to God.

Attitude and motive are both practices that are initiated internally. The results can be seen and heard, but they begin on the inside. This takes us to our third area of study …

3. DYING TO SELF

Matt 16:24,25 "Then Jesus said to his disciples, 'If anyone would come after me, he must deny himself and take up his cross and follow me. For whosoever wants to save his life will lose it, but whoever loses his life for me will find it.'"

Mark 8:34,35 "Then he called the crowds to him along with his disciples and said, 'If anyone would come after me, he must deny himself and take up his cross and follow me. For whoever wants to save his life will lose it, but whoever loses his life for me and for the sake of the gospel will save it. What good is it for a man to gain the whole world, yet forfeit his soul?'"

Luke 9:23,24 "Then he said to them all, 'If anyone would come after me, he must deny himself and take up his cross daily and follow me. For whoever wants to save his life will lose it, but whoever loses his life for me will save it.'"

The battle against self is a daily contest. Our flesh is constantly trying to convince us that 'if it feels good, it must be right.' What did the serpent say in Genesis? "Now the serpent was more crafty than any of the wild animals the Lord God had made. He said to the woman, 'Did God **REALLY** say, You must not eat from any tree in the garden?'

"The woman said to the serpent, 'We may eat from fruit from the trees in the garden, but God did say, 'You must not eat fruit from the tree that is in the middle of the garden, and you must not touch it or you will die.'

"'You will not surely die,' the serpent said to the woman. 'For God knows that when you eat of it, your eyes will be opened and you will be like God, knowing good and evil.'"

Satan accused God of holding out. He implied that God didn't want Eve to enjoy life. But we must remember who our enemy is. He is a liar and a twister of the truth, sometimes ever so subtly.

So when we deny ourselves, we are instead acknowledging God. We are on purpose, deliberately choosing to be self-sacrificing rather than self-serving. Don't think that this is a position of weakness — quite the opposite. When we get ourselves out of the way, God will show Himself in amazing ways.

This daily battle requires us to be steadfast and rooted in the Word. When Jesus was tempted in the desert and the devil tried to get him into the works of the flesh, he replied each time, "It is written." He knew the word and applied it. So must we.

When we choose to sacrifice self, God will provide opportunities for us to bless others. He will help us 'do good on purpose.'

Hebrews 13:15,16 "Through Jesus therefore let us continually offer to God a sacrifice of praise — the fruit of lips that confess his name. And do not forget to do good and to share with others, for with such sacrifices God is pleased."

Galatians 6:10 "Then as we have opportunity, let us do good to all people, especially to those who belong to the family of God."

Galatians 6:2 "Carry each other's burdens, and in this way you will fulfill the law of Christ."

Philippians 2:4-7 "Each of you should look not only to your own interests, but also to the interests of others. Your attitude should be the same as that of Christ Jesus; who being in very nature God, did not consider equality with God something to be grasped, but made himself nothing, taking the very nature of a servant, being made in human likeness."

I trust we'll all remember this the next time we're cut off in traffic or someone takes the spot we'd been waiting for with our signal on at Kroger! We'll have lots of chances to practice!

We have the ability to do this serving and loving and dying to self because of Christ in us.

Luke 6:43 "No good tree bears bad fruit nor does a bad tree bear good fruit. Each tree is recognized by its own fruit. People do not pick figs from thorn bushes or grapes from briers. The good man brings good things out of the good stored up in his heart and the evil man brings evil things out of the evil stored up in his heart. For out of the overflow of his heart his mouth speaks."

There are so many spiritual laws that are paralleled in the natural world around us. God uses seemingly simple examples to showcase profound principles. They appear simple because of their familiarity to us.

One of my favorite parables is the one Jesus told regarding the sower and the seed in the **Luke 8.**

"A farmer went out to sow his seed. As he was scattering the seed, some fell along the path; it was trampled on, and the birds of the air ate it up. Some fell on rock, and when it came up it withered because it had no moisture. Other seed fell among thorns, which grew up with it and choked the plants. Still other seed fell on good soil. It came up and yielded a crop a hundred times more than was sown." The disciples asked the meaning of the parable and he explained, "The seed is the word of God. Those along the path are the ones who hear, and then the devil comes and takes away the word from their hearts, so that they may not believe and be saved. Those on the rock are the ones who receive the word with joy when they hear it, but they have no root. They believe it for a while, but in the time of testing they fall away. The seed that fell among thorns stands for those who hear, but as they go on their way they are choked by life's worries, riches and pleasures, and they do not mature. But the seed on good soil stands for those with a noble and good heart who hear the word, retain it, and by persevering produce a crop."

A seed that receives light and water and the proper soil will **NOT** stay the same. A heart that receives the seed of the word of God **CANNOT** remain unchanged. After a while it may be hard to remember what it used to be like because the fruit that comes from this seed is **LOVE, JOY, PEACE, PATIENCE, KINDNESS, GOODNESS, FAITHFULNESS, GENTLENESS AND GOOD OLD SELF CONTROL!**

And that, girlfriends, is everything we need to have the right attitude, proper and pure motives and win the battle over self!

Let's end on one last wonderful verse:

I Chronicles 28:9 "Serve with wholehearted devotion and with a willing mind for the Lord searched every heart and understands every motive behind the thoughts."

Lesson 2

Last week we studied attitude, motive and dying to self. The scriptures made it clear that who we are begins on the inside. We're all looking forward to that time when we will receive God's praise for the motives of our hearts. We thank you Lord that you help us with the housecleaning that we need to do in order to have pure motives and the proper attitude.

Philippians 1:6 "… He who began a perfect work in you will carry it on to completion until the day of Christ Jesus."

We are not left on our own. God knows the trials we face and also our tendency to shove things under the carpet. I know without a shadow of a doubt that God is just as present in my valleys as he is in my mountaintop moments. Sometimes it feels like we can't see the forest for the trees, but I have found that He is in the trees. Does that make any sense?? Anyway, He keeps teaching me how important it is to 'fess up' when I need to and listen to the prompting of the Holy Spirit.

This brings us to today where we will see how God enables us to overcome opposition and walk in light. They are not mutually exclusive! God has provided the means for us to fight what we need to be opposed to as well as walk in love.

Ephesians 6:10 "Finally, be strong in the Lord and in his mighty power. Put on the full armor of God so that you can take your stand against the devil's schemes. For our struggle is not against flesh and blood, but against the rulers, against the authorities, against the powers of this dark world and against the spiritual forces of evil in the heavenly realms."

This passage makes three points very clear:
1. We have an enemy.
2. It is not flesh and blood, which means we can't see it.
3. We must have God's armor to combat it.

Paul addresses this matter at the end of Ephesians, so to better understand let's look at the beginning of the book. Chapter 1 is sometimes called the Hymn of Grace. Verses 3-14 detail what we have and who we are in Christ.

Read **Ephesians 1:3-14** "We are the body of Christ — Jesus is the head." This is not a ho-hum proposition. For us who believe, we have "his incomparably great power." The same power which God exerted in Christ when he raised him from the dead and seated him at his right hand. This chapter needs to be read and studied and read and studied. The Holy Spirit will give you wisdom and revelation to know him better.

In Chapter 2 we are reminded of who we were and where we are now — then, dead in sin — now, alive in Christ.

Ephesians 2:4,5 "But because of His great love for us, God who is rich in mercy, made us alive with Christ even when we were dead in transgressions — it is by grace you have been saved."

Ephesians 2:8 "For it is by grace you have been saved, through faith and this not from yourselves, it is the gift of God — not by works, so that no one can boast."

So God has done beyond anything we can imagine to reconcile us to Him — his plan of salvation is awesome. But we are not immediately beamed up when we accept Christ and are born again into God's kingdom. We're still here in a world that is dark and hostile to this God that we love. How do we stand against an enemy we cannot see?

Ephesians 6:13 "Therefore put on the full armor of God, so that when (not if — my addition) the day of evil comes, you will be able to stand, and after you have done everything, to stand."

How many of you have been there? I have. And I know for a fact that sometimes we have to just stay put, don't budge, but stand. Standing is a position of confidence as well as defiance to the enemy. It says, "I've taken your best shot, but I'm still standing. And I'm going to keep standing, and I'll tell you how ..."

I have the belt of truth buckled around my waist, the breastplate of righteousness in place, my feet fitted with the readiness that comes from the gospel of peace. In addition to all of that, I take up the shield of faith which will extinguish the flaming darts of the evil one. I take the helmet of salvation and the Word of God.

With my armor in place I am reminded to pray on all occasions and with all kinds of prayers.

God's armor (it's His, and He's letting us use it) is Truth, Righteousness, the Gospel of Peace, Faith, Salvation and His Word.

The Belt of Truth

John 14:5 "I am the way, the truth and the life. No one comes to the Father except through me." Jesus is telling the truth of who He is.

The Breastplate of Righteousness

II Corinthians 5:21 "God made Him who had no sin to be sin for us, so that in Him we might become the righteousness of God."

Feet Fitted with the Gospel of Peace

Isaiah 52:7 "How beautiful on the mountains are the feet of those who bring good news, who proclaim peace, who bring good tidings, who proclaim salvation, who say to Zion, 'Your God reigns!'"

Helmet of Salvation

I Corinthians 1:18 " For the message of the cross is foolishness to those who are perishing, but to us who are being saved it is the power of God."

Shield of Faith

Psalm 91:4 "He will cover you with his feathers and under his wings you will find refuge; his faithfulness will be your shield and rampart."

Sword of the Spirit ... The Word of God

John 1:1,14 "In the beginning was the Word and the Word was with God and the Word was God. The Word became flesh and dwelt among us. We have seen his glory, the glory of the One and Only who came from the Father full of grace and truth."

As we study this and let it sink in, we must remember to pray always. Paul asked the Ephesians to remember to pray for him, "Pray also for me that whenever I open my mouth, words may be given me so that I will fearlessly make known the mystery of the gospel, for which I am an ambassador in chains. Pray that I may declare it fearlessly, as I should."

Twice he uses the word fearlessly. He knew he faced an enemy, and he didn't want to miss an opportunity to proclaim the gospel because he was afraid. But because we feel fear doesn't mean we're not up to the task. The more times I 'do things scared,' the more I see that God has my back. Perfect love cast out fear and God loves me perfectly.

Let's think about how we can be spiritually armed and dangerous and walk in love at the same time. How did Jesus walk? He walked in light — there is no darkness in him.

I John 1:5-7 "This is the message we have heard from him and declare to you: God is light, in Him there is no darkness at all. If we claim to have fellowship with him, yet walk in darkness, we lie and do not live in the truth. But if we walk in the light, as he is in the light, we have fellowship with one another and the blood of Jesus, his Son, purifies us from all sin."

I John 2:5 "This is how we know we are in him; whoever claims to live in him must walk as Jesus walked."

This wonderful lesson is certainly one that is easily understood. Go into a strange room, turn off all the lights and try to navigate from one side to the other. I used the word strange because our journey is made up of brand new unknown todays. We don't know what this day will bring. So you may have memorized the pattern of yesterday, but it will do you no good today. And if you are insistent on pursuing the path as you think it is laid out, as it seems right to you, you will surely stumble.

The Old Testament is so exciting because we are able to see who the Messiah is — his character, his purpose, his uniqueness that sets him apart. The prophets detailed descriptions of his birth and life and death and resurrection are stunning. We're looking at just one part of who Christ is from the many names that he is called ... **LIGHT!**

Psalm 27:1: "The Lord is my light and my salvation — whom shall I fear?"

Psalm 36:9: "For with you is the fountain of life; in your light we see light."

Psalm 43:3: "Send forth your light and your truth and let them guide me."

Psalm 119:105: "Your word is a lamp unto my feet and a light unto my path."

Proverbs 4:18: "The path of the righteous is like the first gleam of dawn shining ever brighter until the full light of day." (Just like our walk keeps getting brighter.)

Ecclesiastes 11:7: "Light is sweet and it pleases the eyes to see the sun." (Nothing like a sunny day to lift your spirits — topped only by a sunny day **AND** the light of God shining in our hearts)

Isaiah 9:2: "The people walking in darkness have seen a great light; on those living in the land of the shadow of death a light has dawned." (We are living in a world that is under a death sentence and into that miserable darkness a Light has come!)

Now what does the New Testament say concerning light — specifically Matthew and John.

Matthew 5:14-16: Jesus is speaking. "You are the light of the world. A city on a hill cannot be hidden.

Neither do people light a lamp and put it under a bowl. Instead they put it on its stand, and it gives light to everyone in the house. In the same way let your light shine before men that they may see your good deeds and praise your Father in heaven."

John 1:4-9: "In him was life and that life was the light of men. The light shines in the darkness, but the darkness has not understood it. There came a man who was sent from God; his name was John. He came as a witness to testify concerning light; so that through him all men might believe. He himself was not the light; he came only to witness to the light. The true light that gives light to every man was coming into the world."

John 3:16: "For God so loved the world that he gave his only begotten Son that whosoever believes in him shall not perish, but have eternal life. For God did not send his Son into the world to condemn the world, but to save the world through him. Whoever believes in him is not condemned, but whoever does not believe stands condemned already because he has not believed in the name of God's one and only Son. This is the verdict: Light has come into the world, but men loved darkness instead of light, because their deeds were evil. Everyone who does evil hates the light and will not come to the light for fear that his deeds will be exposed. But whoever lives by the truth comes into the light, so that it may be seen plainly that what he has done has been done through God."

Let me close by telling a story about light shining in darkness. While on a trip to Nepal, my sister and her husband visited a leprosy hospital called Anandaban Hospital. The sign outside the entrance read:

Most Important Visitor

People affected by leprosy are the most important
visitors on our premises.
They are not dependent on us —
we are dependent on them.
Service to them is the purpose of our work.
They are not outsiders to our service.
They are part of it.
We are not doing them favor by serving them.
They are giving us an opportunity.

Barb and Charles were so moved by the sign that
they copied down the words. As they were taken
through the hallways, it was apparent that the patients
were indeed the most important ones there.

The last room that they visited was one they will
never forget. The door was opened, and there was an
elderly woman sitting on a mat reading. She had been
a patient at the hospital but now her leprosy was in
remission. But because of the disease, her family had
rejected her and she had no place to go. She was given
permission to stay at the hospital and had been there
for 40 years!

They stepped into her room, and Barb said there
was peace and light that filled it. They prayed with her
and then she prayed for them. Even though they couldn't
understand her language, the power of her words could
not be mistaken.

When they left, she went back to her Bible and the
book of Jeremiah that she had been reading before her
visitors came.

12

William Rose

My husband loved a story with a happy ending. I found this out early in our marriage when we went to see *Love Story* with Ali MacGraw and Ryan O'Neal. This popular book-turned movie was drawing large audiences in 1970. Because I had read the novel, I was interested in seeing how it would translate to the big screen.

My reluctant partner joined me and spent the next two hours regretting his decision. While I swabbed my eyes with tissues, he was asking himself why someone would voluntarily sit through this kind of "entertainment." He remained steadfast in his movie choices, preferring intrigue and action, but no sad endings please. We may be one of the few couples who never saw *Titanic* because in his words, "You know what happens, and it's not good!"

I still remember sitting with him at the IU auditorium for the much anticipated (on my part) production of *Les Miserables*. He made it through to the intermission (I called it halftime) and then excused himself to go to the office. I must say the second half was more enjoyable without the person beside me sighing and squirming in his seat! When he picked me up afterwards, I was still euphoric with the music replaying in my head. He was pleased that he had caught up on correspondence that he hadn't had time to do. We laughed on the way home about how some things never change.

Terry was also known in our family as someone who could not watch anything that involved children being hungry or mistreated. He couldn't get to the remote fast enough to change the channel if a program dealt with little ones in need. I think he struggled with the unfairness of it and his perceived inability to do anything about it. It was easier to just not think about it.

Several months before Terry died he was resting in bed. I was in the room as well, but was occupied with sorting laundry or some other kind of chore. The television was on and the program was one showing children in a third world setting waiting in line for food. I was only half listening when I heard Terry say something. "I want to do that."

Thinking I had misunderstood him, I reminded him that we donated to the organization and even though we weren't there physically, we were helping to provide for them. "No, I want to **DO** that," he said. I looked at him and said, "You want to actually feed children?" And he replied, "Yes, I do."

His tone left no room to doubt his sincerity. It's hard for me to describe the power of that moment. Terry's heart was at such a different place. He was able to look past the uncomfortable situation he was in at that moment and recognize someone else's need. II Corinthians 4:16 says: "Though outwardly we are wasting away, yet inwardly we are being renewed day by day."

Like it or not, as we age it begins to happen to us all. But at the same time inwardly, in our spirit, we're becoming more alive in Christ. I was seeing this contrast right before me. God has a heart for his hungry children and Terry was seeing that need through the Father's eyes. He wasn't changing the channel, he was asking to be used. I felt privileged to have witnessed this example of what God will do for us if we allow Him to be a part of our lives.

More than a year after Terry passed away, my sister, Barbara, called to tell me about a mission trip she had decided to take. She would be going to Ukraine with a small team of volunteers from all over the country. Her excitement was apparent as she went through the litany of places they would visit — orphanages, boarding schools, baby hospitals. There was a pause in the conversation and I said, "I'm going!" I could hear the smile in her voice when she said, "You're going because of what Terry said, aren't you?" She was absolutely right. I was going for him as well as for me.

Once again I was heading into uncharted waters and attempting something that I never dreamed I would be doing. But God was opening doors and providing opportunities that were just what I needed. It was motivating for me to know that Terry would be pleased and somehow I sensed that encouragement. There was much to be done and I eagerly began making lists hoping that I would not forget anything. My family and friends were so supportive. It was another reinforcement for me of how important relationships are. I couldn't have done it without them.

Our team consisted of 14 volunteers. We were representing GAiN which stands for Global Aid Network and is affiliated with Campus Crusade. Four of us were first timers or "newbies" as we were called and had no concept of what awaited us.

Because we were from all over the country — California to Virginia — we communicated primarily by email. We were also informed that there would be two conference calls which would give us an opportunity to "meet" our teammates. The first call was on a Friday evening at 8 p.m. We were told to block off an hour of time and find a quiet place to avoid interruptions. I stationed myself in a comfy chair at my desk with my cup of coffee close at hand.

I had printed off the agenda of items that we would be discussing and began going over it. I still had a few minutes before I had to make the call. As I scanned the page my eyes stopped on the name of the person responsible for the media. William Rose. That name had no significance for anyone except me. For privacy reasons Terry was admitted to Bloomington Hospital under an assumed name. The name chosen for him was William Rose! Hospital staff would come into the room and ask, "Should we call him Mr. Rose? William? Bill?" We would answer, "How about Coach?"

And now to be looking at that name that was a part of this trip to "feed children" was awe-inspiring. It was not a coincidence, but a hug from God just for me. From that moment I looked forward to meeting William Rose and wondered what he would be like.

As it turned out, Bill was a retired English teacher from Colfax, California. He and his wife Adele had traveled to Ukraine many times and were such great examples of walking out one's faith. While I knew I would tell him how meaningful his name was to me, I wasn't quite sure when would be the appropriate time.

We met at JFK airport, and I was at once struck by his keen intellect and gentle spirit. But I had to chuckle at God's sense of humor. This William Rose didn't have an athletic bone in his body! I waited until we had been in Ukraine for several days before I told my story to him and the others.

After our evening meal time was allotted for sharing about anything special that had happened that day. On this particular night I looked at Barb and knew she was thinking the same thought I was. And so everyone in that little room heard about William Rose and why that name and person would always have such a special place in my heart. There wasn't a dry eye when I finished, but we all got a reminder of how much God cares for us even down to the smallest details. When our trip was over, several people on the team told me that though they had never met Terry, they felt like they had come to know him through the time we had spent together.

The trip to Ukraine in March of 2009 was such a blessing in so many ways. To be able to experience it with my sister made it even more memorable. With the demands of family and other obligations, we had stayed close by phone calls and occasional visits. Now we were roommates and traveling companions.

We arrived in New York City the day before our departure date to give ourselves a cushion of time and also to have a chance to enjoy the city. Two women, Michelle and Marilyn, from Barb's home town of Bay Minette, Ala., were also members of our team. The four of us walked through Central Park and along 5th Avenue to the Metropolitan Museum of Art. We spent the afternoon exploring and becoming acquainted as we walked. Unfortunately, Michelle and I had worn boots that provided warmth, but not comfort. We would have to stop every now and then to give our feet a rest.

Judging from the amount of laughter coming from these four women, you might have thought they were lifelong friends. The bond that we shared was immediate and I was thankful that they would be with me for this adventure. After a late dinner and an entertaining cab ride to the hotel, we were ready for bed.

We arrived at JFK airport four hours before our departure. This gave us plenty of time to meet everyone and cope with any unexpected wrinkles. (My husband called it planning for the unexpected!) The most difficult aspect of this trip was knowing I couldn't pick up my phone and call my kids. Making those final calls at the airport was a struggle. My children are such a source of encouragement, and I was sad to think of not hearing those voices everyday. There were many thoughts swirling around in my mind as we taxied away from all that was familiar to me and headed into the unknown.

Our plane reached Prague at 6 a.m. and we had a four hour layover before the final leg to Odessa. Everyone was encouraged to adapt to the new time zone as quickly as possible. I was now operating on a seven hour time difference with Indiana, but was told not to think about it as we acclimated to our new schedule. Easier said than done! Our arrival at the hotel in Odessa was close to the dinner hour.

We had our first official Chicken Kiev and had to fight through the urge to fall asleep at the table. We received instructions regarding our morning departure and headed to our rooms. As we looked out from our balcony, the sights and sounds were unfamiliar yet had a beauty that comes from such a rich history. This landscape would become etched in my memory as the next 10 days unfolded.

The following morning began as all of our days would: with a team devotional. Each day one person was responsible for leading this quiet time, and we quickly recognized the importance of this routine. This was another way that we got to know each other and the variety of backgrounds and personalities were clear. Each life story was unique in its journey, yet we had all experienced God's love and forgiveness. This common thread would become stronger as we worked together and began to see how each of our talents complimented one another.

After one night in Odessa, we departed by bus to Kherson. As we drove through the city, we passed many empty buildings and deserted factories. Our guide, Oksana, pointed out the catacombs where Jewish people hid during the occupation by Nazi Germany.

Leaving the city behind, we traveled through the countryside to reach our destination in the southeastern part of Ukraine. At the end of that day my journal entry concluded, "Thank you, Jesus, for giving us life that is worth living. You have brought me to this place — Ukraine! Who would've thought?!!"

Each morning after breakfast we loaded the bus with our 'goodies' that we would be distributing that day. Besides the GAiN boxes packed with much-needed supplies, we each had backpacks that were filled with our personal gifts for the children and workers. At times I thought we might fall over backward because of the weight of the load. I felt some empathy for the plight of turtles! Our team was divided into groups of four, each with its own interpreter. As we visited each location, the value of Alla, our interpreter, became apparent. She was literally our link to everyone we met and our appreciation could not be overstated.

Our first visit was to a baby house, and my group was sent to the one- and two-year-old area. I stood there thinking that this room was these little ones entire world. It was where they ate, slept and played. After passing out the gifts, it was obvious that the stuffed bear that each child received was the hands-down favorite. This would be the case at each location, even when teenagers were the recipients. It was a very tangible gift of love. Baby Anya and I seemed to connect as we sat on the floor and played with her new stuffed animal. Her face remains in my memory.

After each visit our team leader would ask the director about their most pressing need. Then, as we sat on the bus, he would relay to us what the staff person had said. We would then pass the hat (literally) and each of us had the opportunity to give for that particular need. The money that was collected was given to a responsible person who would see to it that it was used for the intended purpose.

GAiN has a long history of partnering with local people of integrity, and I saw how important this is. During the next 10 days our hat-passing would provide money for food, gas, electricity, furniture, clothes dryer, medicine, bedding, shoes, and a computer. I was finding out how rewarding it is to give!

That afternoon we went to a Children's Hospital. As we were led through old hallways and dimly lit corridors, it was hard not to compare this place to hospitals that I was used to. We got to go into rooms with babies and their mothers to give them the gifts we brought as well as the beaded bracelets that explained the gospel message. To say I felt inadequate is an understatement. Here I saw people taking care of sick, innocent little ones in spite of the surroundings. They were doing the best they could with what they had.

My journal entry that day read, "Nothing could have prepared me for our trip to the Children's Hospital. As we entered the small crib-filled room, I couldn't get past Igor. Paralysis kept his little hands curled by his face and his legs lay in an uncomfortable looking position. But those eyes … those eyes are in my heart forever. As I caressed his face and sang *Jesus Loves Me* to him, it struck me that God looks at us with such deep love and compassion. Although Igor was unable to speak, I know he felt the presence of the Holy Spirit. I'm praying that I'll get to see Igor again in heaven — running and laughing and playing with the other children."

The final stop on the first day was at a shelter for runaway children. They ranged in ages from four to 16. Once more it was a heart-breaking scenario. These were children who were living on the streets because they had been abandoned by their parents. The shelter was a temporary home for them until they could be placed in a boarding school. It was a constantly revolving door.

It was impossible for me not to think of my Tucker, Spencer, Tate and Quinn when I looked at children that were about their age. We gathered in a large room where we began our presentation with a map showing where each of us lived and how far we had come to visit them. I sat next to Alonya and hoped that somehow she would understand how much God loved her and had a purpose for her life. As we left we heard knocking coming from the window above the entrance. There were some of the children waving and blowing kisses. I'll never be the same again. That night at dinner I shared the William Rose story.

The experiences of the first day would be repeated nine more times. To re-live each of them on these pages would be emotionally-wrenching, but there are two other encounters that deserve to be told. It's my hope that these stories will not only tug at your heart strings, but inspire you as well.

On our visit to a boarding school for disabled children we found ourselves surrounded by young people in wheelchairs and on walkers and crutches. They listened intently to our presentation, and we enjoyed the smiles as we passed out the goody bags and bears. We mingled and chatted with the boys and girls, trying to talk with as many as possible. The interpreters were working hard to keep up with us.

There was a woman at the back of the room and I made my way to her. An interpreter was next to her and on the other side was a 13-year-old child named Olga. The woman was from the state of Washington and her family was adopting Olga. They had adopted a son from Ukraine several years earlier and decided to do it again. This time, though, they were looking for someone that they didn't think anyone else would want.

Because of a birth defect, Olga's arms stopped just below her shoulders. Her life will not be an easy one, but she is part of a family that loves her and wants her. It was another amazing moment as I thought about the opportunity and hope that Olga had been given. I am in awe of such acts of love and selflessness. Some people will say, "Why go half way around the world when there is need here?" I say that the need is great everywhere and wherever we can help is the place we should be.

The second story is about a ministry to the homeless children of Kherson called House of Hope. What is now a daycare shelter with meals served and classes taught, began when one woman refused to look away.

Galina Kuleshova came across a child who had died and was lying on the steps of the pedestrian subway. No one else stopped. The passersby continued on their way. Her life changed in that moment when she climbed out of her comfort zone. Enlisting the help of a friend, she began taking bread and milk to the kids on the streets. They eventually found themselves going into sewers where runaways lived in the network of underground pipes.

After four years of street ministry, they met Pastor

Andrey who shared their vision for these young people. From this partnership House of Hope began. Our GAiN team was privileged to meet Galina and Pastor Andrey when they came to talk to us after dinner one evening. Here was a woman who was incredibly beautiful on the outside, but that beauty was overshadowed by her inner strength and love for God. She was passionate about these children and tireless in her efforts to feed and care for them. As our team listened to their stories, we asked if we might join them in taking food to the ones living in the sewers.

It was agreed that we would go on Friday evening. Several of our team members opted not to go, and I completely understood. I wasn't too sure how it would affect me. We drove to a roundabout in the middle of the city and parked on the grassy area in the middle. (Driving etiquette is much different in Kherson with no thought given to parking on sidewalks or in the middle of roundabouts!) We walked to where a manhole cover had been removed to reveal an opening in the ground.

Several people began to go down the ladder in the hole. I debated for a moment, but decided to do it. As I lowered myself down, it was dark and I was glad there were friends waiting at the bottom with a flashlight. No one was there, but trash and garbage was everywhere. It was obvious from the smell that someone had been sick. There was a huge pipe carrying hot water for the city running through the sewer and it provided heat for those living there. We tried to take in what we were seeing, but even now it's hard to describe.

It wasn't long until one of the people who lived there arrived. He told us he was embarrassed because his area had been vandalized, and he hadn't had a chance to tidy up. He told us his story and sadly it had a familiar ring to it. He had been in an orphanage until he was 18 and at that age you are on your own. He had no family and no place to go except where we were standing. This was his home. We prayed with him and left food and candles, but we all went away with heavy hearts.

As all of these experiences made their way into my heart and mind, I found myself with lots to ponder. What did God have in store for me? What was my purpose? How would these experiences change me? All of these thoughts were rolling around in my head as our team prepared to start our trip back to the US.

I felt such affection for the people with whom I had worked the last two weeks. At the farewell breakfast for our interpreters, we had a chance to thank them and give them some gifts as tokens of our appreciation. Each of them had the opportunity to address the group, and it was humbling to hear how devoted they were to building the kingdom of God. They were grateful for the part they had played in serving others. Sergey Pereversev said it best. "The blessing would not be so great if we deserved it." I wrote it down on a napkin and have kept it as a reminder of my Ukrainian brothers and sisters.

My trip home took longer than expected due to delays and cancelled flights. By the time I got to Bloomington, I was exhausted and wondered if I could do this again. For right now I was content with being home and hearing my precious children's voices again.

13

Terry's Favorite Play

I'm sure all football fans have their favorite play. For some it's the long touchdown pass. For others it's the interception that's returned for a score. Some live for that momentum-changing sack or that big hit over the middle.

Without a doubt Terry's favorite play was 'Take a Knee.' At that point, he was taking off his headphones and looking up at the scoreboard watching the clock tick away the final few seconds. It was 'game over.' The exhilarating feeling of accomplishment made the 60minute struggle worthwhile. It was confirmation that a victory had been won.

It might surprise some to know that Terry didn't like to use the word 'victory'... he preferred 'win.' He thought victory should be used in a spiritual context, because it described something much bigger than a game. The ultimate victory is the one we experience as believers.

Hopefully, that message has come through clearly in this book. We live victoriously when we trust God and the plan that He has for our lives. He's not only the architect, but the producer and director as well. And because it's His script, we can be comfortable knowing it will all work out. We have his word on it: Romans 8:28 "For we know that all things work together for good for those who love God and are called according to his purpose." That gives me confidence to stay the course and not allow myself to quit.

When I think of Terry's final days, I think about how he 'took a knee' that morning in Bloomington Hospital. And as he did it, with the clock counting down, he was thinking in terms of a victory, not a win. I believe with all certainty that he is part of a celebration right now that is unlike any he ever experienced here.

In keeping with the football analogies, I would describe my life as in the 'clock management' phase. I need to handle the ball. Don't lose it or fumble it away. Those parallels are quite appropriate. While I am certainly working my way toward the 'take a knee' play, my thoughts are focused on the things I need to be doing in the meanwhile.

There was a movie released in 2007 called "The Bucket List" with Morgan Freeman and Jack Nicholson. I didn't see it, but am familiar with the storyline. Two cancer patients make a list of all the things they want to do before they die. Learn to paint. Travel to places they've never been. Try skydiving or some such dangerous feat. It's an interesting concept and understandable when given their circumstances.

What would happen if we would have a 'spiritual bucket' that would be a wish list for all of those daring acts we'd like to do for God before we die? It gives me pause when I think of my life in those terms. I'm not a goal-setter like my husband was, but I'm finding that I am open to possibilities when they present themselves.

The trip to Ukraine is a perfect example. It was never on my radar screen or to-do list. But I found myself wanting to participate and sensing that it was where I was supposed to go. In hindsight I can see how many circumstances had to line up in order for me to be a part of that mission trip. I can honestly say that for me it was a daring feat! Do I have a list of nine other spiritual goals that I want to accomplish before I die? Probably not. But I think that God does and they'll happen in a way and time that is His choosing. My only obligation is to be willing. In the meanwhile my goal is to remain focused and headed in the right direction.

I'm experiencing a kind of freedom right now that I've never known. It comes as a direct result of being widowed, and consequently the liberty is bittersweet. For the first time in my life I don't have the obligation of being a spouse or a coach's wife. All of the energies that went into to those roles are no longer needed. But the energy is still there.

When I understood the enormity of this void, I decided to do something to fill it. I looked at what interested me and what I was drawn to. Our son Drew had been involved with Young Life when he was in high school and as a leader when he was at Miami University. I always had a soft spot in my heart for this organization and their ministry of sharing God's love with teenagers.

I contacted Jeff Mahrt who is the person in charge of the Bloomington chapter and asked to see him. Over our Starbuck's coffee I explained my situation and told him that I wanted to be a part of Young Life in whatever capacity he thought best.

I became a member of the Care Team which oversees the various needs, helps with event planning and provides prayer support. I also volunteered my house for monthly leadership meetings for the IU students. The "lady" leaders use my house for slumber parties each semester, and it brings back memories of Amy and Allison's earlier years! If I needed confirmation about the correctness of getting involved with YL, God provided it beautifully as you will see.

When my home sold, I began searching for a place that would be just right. After going through four or five houses, I knew when I walked into the next one that I was home. I made an offer on it and when it came back from the sellers, there was a note attached. "Tell Jane that we know Drew."

Chris and Tracy Berry were selling their house and moving back to Cincinnati. Tracy had Drew in Young Life Leadership Training while at Miami before they had moved to Bloomington. As it turned out the position I filled on the Care Team was the one vacated by Chris. Once again I was in awe of God's care and timing.

I would also become involved with the Hannah House/Crisis Pregnancy Center. Several years earlier Terry and I had received an invitation to a fundraiser in the mail. I kept the card for a long time, wishing that I had the time to volunteer for them. I felt a connection that I didn't quite understand until later.

I was approached several months after Terry died about the possibility of speaking at the Hannah House Gala in November. When I met with the director she told me the back story regarding why they asked me to speak. Their original choice had been Terry. Even though he couldn't do it, she kept going back to his name and couldn't seem to get him out of her mind. On a whim she contacted me to see if there was any chance that I would be interested.

I thought back to the tug at my heart that I had felt two years before and now knew the reason for it. I accepted the offer to be their speaker as well to serve as to serve as a board member. God had opened another door for me and welcomed me in.

When we contemplate the idea of 'clock management,' we must remember that there is indeed a clock. We need to get our minds around the fact that each of us has a beginning and an end in this life.

Everything that Terry and I went through has made me so aware of the reality of this. Many people avoid thinking about it because it's frightening if you don't know where you're going. The good news is that Jesus provided a way for every single one of us. We don't have to be afraid. When we believe by faith that he is who he says he is and can do what he says he can do, we've started down that path of victory.

The farther I go on this path, the more I realize that nothing I do can change God's love for me. Instead of being afraid, it makes me want to please Him and enjoy my Heavenly Father. I heard someone recently put it this way, "God doesn't need us. He wants us!" I can't think of a better way to say it.

For some people it's difficult to reconcile how a God who loves us could allow us to suffer pain and loss. There were many people with questions of 'why' when Terry died. My children asked the same questions, and we all still want what's missing.

I recently found an email that my sister sent me not long after Terry passed away. I'm sure I read it at the time, but it means more to me now. It's from a devotional by David Hazzard addressing this topic of questioning God's motives: John 3:12 "I have spoken to you of earthly things and you do not believe; how then will you believe when I speak of heavenly things?"

"God has far less interest in temporal dominion and in temporal freedom — The Spirit and the eternal kingdom are first. So do not be deceived into interpreting the promises and instructions of our Lord without taking into account the heights and depths of his Spirit. To try to limit His words only to what we can understand is like attempting to grasp the air. Yes, you might succeed in snatching some small particle that is borne on the wind—but how can you trap the air itself in your hands?

It is important for a man, if he is not truly spiritual, to comprehend how God is arranging and governing circumstances. Let me give you a few examples so that you will more clearly understand.

Suppose a Christian man falls into the hand of enemies, who abuse and persecute him. He cries out to God, and God answers, saying, 'I will set you free from all your enemies.' This word may well be true and yet his captors may continue in their own wickedness and he may die at their hands.

Now if he or his friends expected God's answer to come in terms of temporal freedom, they would have deceived themselves. For God may have meant that the man's deliverance would be that final, complete freedom – heaven where there is full victory over this life. When God speaks, we must assume that He is referring first to the things that are most profitable and most important, and that is the life of the Spirit."

Reading and studying that passage two years after Terry's passing has reinforced for me that his life as well as his death were in God's hands. There are no pat answers and to try to provide any would be foolish. But it would be equally foolish to stop pursuing God, and by doing so, miss all that He has in store for us. I believe that the hard knocks give us the most opportunity for growth if we allow them to.

Tom Ellsworth, my pastor at Sherwood Oaks Christian Church, asked in a sermon several weeks ago, "Are you wearing a bib or are you wearing an apron?" In other words, do you need to be bottle-fed and have someone attend to your every need? And if things don't go your way, do you throw a fit until you get what you want? Or have you taken off that bib and put on an apron to serve?

When you've put the apron on and you're serving others, you are not concerned about serving yourself. There's a reason that the first of the Ten Commandments says, "You shall have no other gods before me."

Sometimes that god is self, me, I and we don't want to part with it. But God cautions us over and over about what happens when we put 'things' before Him. It causes a separation and we're the cause of it, not God. He doesn't go anywhere, we do. That's why it's important for us to examine our hearts and our motives and get rid of anything that is keeping us from a right relationship with God. Hopefully you won't be as stubborn as I was and take 20 years to repay the florist's bill!

Writing this book has been a blessing for me. It has given me the opportunity to look at my life and gain a new appreciation for how God has "made my path straight." And along that road He has brought many people who have offered friendship and encouragement. You've read about many of them in these pages, but there are countless others who touched our lives as well. From many different walks of life they came when we needed them the most. I've referred to them as 'hugs from God,' and they continue to be sent my way.

That brings me to one more story that I wanted to make sure was included in my book. I simply call it "The Wallet Story."

Sometime after Christmas, 2006, Terry lost his wallet. We looked everywhere for it. He sometimes kept it in the console of the car and always put it in a certain drawer when he came into the house. It was neither place.

He searched his desk at the office as well as at home. The more we looked, the more we kept coming up empty. There was snow on the ground and we thought that maybe when it melted we would find it in the driveway or in the parking lot at the football offices.

I had people all over praying for us to find that wallet! We had an Adidas Clinic to attend in Las Vegas in February, and he was determined that he would find his license by then. But he didn't. I cancelled the credit cards, and he got a new driver's license.

I would think about it every now and then and continued to look in the same places we had searched dozens of times. Someone was always asking if we had found the wallet. And the answer was over and over again, no. Spring came, the snow melted and there was not a sign of his wallet. With our concern about Terry's health, thoughts of the missing billfold all but disappeared.

A year and a half later I moved to my new house. While packing boxes and sorting through things to donate, the question of the missing wallet came up again. We wondered if it would turn up in the process of emptying drawers and going through cabinets. It didn't, and we forgot about it. I was settled into my new surroundings at the end of September, 2008.

On October 15th, I was speaking to a hospital foundation group in Greenfield, Indiana. This town is located about 20 miles east of Indianapolis. Allison had gone with me from Bloomington, and we were seated with family and friends who had come to be with us.

Shortly before the program was to start I saw the woman who was in charge of the program talking to Allison. She suddenly turned to me, and there were tears in her eyes. "They found dad's wallet!"

It didn't make sense and I asked her to repeat herself. It seems that there was a woman at the dinner who was on the foundation board and her daughter was a student at IU. She and some of her friends were going on a weekend retreat and went to the Bloomington Goodwill Store to look for comfortable sweat pants.

As they were looking through the men's rack of clothing, she reached into a pocket and pulled out a wallet. She opened it and immediately realized whose wallet it was. She ran out of the store with it trying to figure out what to do.

She saw the address on his license, but thought it would be too sad to give it to me that way. (What she didn't know at the time was that I had moved and was no longer living at the address any way). Her next thought was to call her mother and ask her advice.

This was taking place on a Friday. She explained the dilemma to her mother, who said, "Believe it or not, I'm going to a dinner next week where Jane Hoeppner is speaking, and I can tell her about it then. I'll give her your number and you can get together with her." So the mother had relayed the message that had been given to Allison. There wasn't a dry eye at our table.

Josiah Sears, who had played football at Greenfield-Central before coming to IU, introduced me that night. I told the crowd that I was a little weak-kneed because of what had just happened.

For all of those events and people to be in the right place at the right time is more than coincidence. And just as unbelievable was how many times we went through clothes checking pockets! Those pants were in the closet until they went to the Goodwill Store when I moved.

I couldn't wait until the next day when I would meet Briana and try to tell her how grateful I was that she was the one who found Coach's wallet. I took her a copy of *Hep Remembered*, a hat and note of thanks enclosed with a small reward for her honesty. She didn't want to take the money, but I insisted. She was so sweet, just like I thought she would be.

Several days later I received a thank you from her and noticed the return address. She lived on Woodburn St. Woodburn is the name of the town that Terry was from! I still have the letter and was especially struck by one thing she wrote. "Things happen for a reason" was one of Terry's favorite sayings.

The next week I was at football practice talking to some of the athletic staff. One of the coaches walked up and said, "Did you hear about that girl that came to the Varsity Club? The one who found Coach's wallet?"

She had taken the money I had given her and donated it in Coach's name for the North End Zone Project at Memorial Stadium. This project had been part of Terry's vision for Indiana football.

It's an incredible story that continues to bless people every time I tell it. And the wallet ... it's in a special place where I can pick it up and hold it and be reminded of God's goodness.

Terry successfully executed his favorite play on June 19th, 2007, when he put his knee down for the final time. Someday I'll have that same thrill to 'Take a Knee' and rejoin him in another place. The thought of that is very exciting to me. In the meantime there is much to do as I listen for God's whisper and trust His plan for my life.

Of one thing I am confident: I will never, **EVER,** quit.

Epilogue

When Terry Hutchens approached me in 2007 about doing a book, I declined. While I knew it was a story that people wanted to hear, it was too soon for me to begin writing about it. I gave my blessing to Hutch's endeavor and was pleased when *'Hep Remembered'* came out in the fall of that year. That book retold stories about Terry from many of his colleagues, players and friends. He did a great job capturing all that was Coach Hep.

This book was a labor of love and gratefulness for the legacy that I have been left. Proverbs 22:1 says, "A good name is more desirable than great riches; to be esteemed is better than silver or gold." My husband gave me the priceless gift of his good reputation. He also gave me three children who will forever miss their dad and his strong presence in their lives. Terry's traits and characteristics live on in Tucker, Spence, Tate and Quinny. Each one of them is a comfort to me and has helped to heal my heart.

Looking closely at my life has also let me see how God has provided friends for me at each stop along the way. From Eva to Kalynn to Karen and Doretta, I know they were hand-picked just for me and me for them. I am thankful for the coaching families that have always been a part of our extended family.

Examining my path since June of 2007 has let me see that progress has been made. Those anniversaries bring more smiles than tears, and we have used the memories as a source of strength. On the second anniversary of Terry's death, my grandson Spencer was with me in Bloomington.

I decided we were going to make it a fun day that my grandson would remember. We packed our lunch, brought along beach towels to sit on and stopped at the florist shop on the way to the cemetery. Spence helped me pick out four perfect red and white roses for Pa from his four little guys. Allison joined us for lunch, and we talked and laughed as we retold stories about her dad and Spencer's Pa. We even played some games of Crazy Eights before it was time to go. As always, we talked about how much fun it's going to be when we're all together again!

My life at this time may not be quite as exciting as it was with Terry, but I am learning that there is a marked difference between having joy and being happy. Happiness comes from the word 'happenstance' which infers that something must occur in order to achieve it. If I have to depend on events that are pleasing to me in order to be happy, there will be lots of highs and lows. I'm not saying that we shouldn't enjoy the highlights along the journey, only that they will fall short of giving us any kind of lasting contentment.

Joy and peace are what God provides for his children, and they go deep where circumstances can't affect them. I know this is true, because I have lived it. It is described this way in Psalm 131, "But I have stilled and quieted my soul; like a weaned child is my soul within me." When I read this, the words jumped out at me, because as a mother I know the difference between the behavior of a weaned child and one who is not. One who is still dependent on her mother's milk can be almost frantic until she is satisfied. But a weaned child can be held by its mother and nurtured without the insistence of being fed. This is part of how God 'grows us up.'

As a coach's wife I saw first hand how conditional love works. There is no one held in greater regard than someone who wins lots of games and keeps the losses to a minimum. But it was quite an awakening for Terry when he realized that football was what he did, not who he was. It didn't mean that he worked any less, on the contrary his worth ethic was never doubted. It helped him realize that his most important obligation was to his players and making them the best young men they could be.

As a believer I have seen how unconditional love works. God's love for me is not based on how many 'wins and losses' I have or what a success or failure I have been. We don't have to clean ourselves up before we're acceptable to Him. When we turn around and run to Him, He'll pick us up, brush us off and put us on the right path. And He'll do it again, and again and again.

I pray this book has been an encouragement to you. God wants you to know that He has a plan for you and it's good. He said so in his word. "For I know the plans I have for you," says the Lord, "plans to prosper you and not to harm you, plans to give you hope and a future."

I also pray that you trust Him. He will strengthen you to never, EVER, quit!

Scripture References

The following is a compilation of verses that have been useful to me. I have noted the dates that appear in my Bible beside some of them, and I am reminded of how they spoke to what I was going through at that time.

I am not a professional Bible scholar and the categories are not etched in stone. You will find that some of the verses could have been listed under more than one heading. The category that I call "God's Awesomeness" contains scriptures that reveal His greatness and are wonderful to ponder. The "How to Live" section lists verses that address ways that will help you in the day-to-day grind of walking out your faith. May these words encourage you to take off that bib and put on your apron!

BE STRONG

Joshua 1:9
I Chronicles 28:9
Esther 4:14
Psalm 16:7,8 — 6/23/07
Psalm 27:1 — 1/13/06
Psalm 118:17
Psalm 119:111,112 — 12/3/07
Psalm 130:5-8 — 12/5/07
Psalm 147:10,11 — 3/15/08
Proverbs 21:30,31
Isaiah 12:2
Isaiah 28:31
Isaiah 40:31
Isaiah 51:8
Isaiah 54:4,5 — 4/16/08
Zechariah 12:5
John 10:10
Acts 20:24 — 2/12/07
Philippians 1:6, 28-30
Ephesians 6:10-20

COMFORT

Psalm 119:50 — 5/18/08
Psalm 147:3
Ecclesiastes 3:11
Isaiah 61:3
Jeremiah 31:16,17
Naham 1:17
II Corinthians 1:4
II Corinthians 4:16
I Thessalonians 4:13

GOD'S AWESOMENESS

Psalm 4:7
Psalm 30:12
Psalm 100
Psalm 118:22-24
Psalm 131:2
Ecclesiastes 11:15
Isaiah 9
Isaiah 40:3-5
Isaiah 52-7
Isaiah 53
Isaiah 55:11 — 9/25/07
Isaiah 61:7-11
Zephaniah 3:9, 17
Luke 11:11-13
Luke 15:7, 10
John 3:16-21
Romans 2:4 — 5/14/09
Romans 3:22-24
Romans 4:17-25
Romans 5:5
Romans 6:3,4, 11
Romans 8:28 — 1/4/06
Romans 8:37
II Corinthians 5:21
Galatians 2:21
Ephesians 1:3, 17-20
Ephesians 2:4, 8, 14
Ephesians 3:6
Colossians 1:21
Hebrews 11:6
James 5:11, 14-16
I Peter 1:3-9
Revelation 12:11

HOW TO LIVE

Job 6:24
Psalm 36:1,2 — 5/9/06
Psalm 84:10
Psalm 86:11-13 — 8/19/08
Psalm 94:12,13
Psalm 119:11
Psalm 119:29-32 — 3/09
Psalm 119:33-39 — 5/08
Psalm 119:67 — 5/14/09
Psalm 119:71
Proverbs 2:9, 12
Proverbs 3:7,8 — 4/13/07
Proverbs 3:13
Proverbs 4:20-27
Proverbs 6:16-19
Proverbs 10:22, 2
Proverbs 11:3, 5
Proverbs 12:28, 30
Proverbs 20:11
Proverbs 22:19, 20
Proverbs 23:17, 18
Proverbs 28:13, 23
Proverbs 30:8,9
Proverbs 31:11,12
Ecclesiastes 5:7
Ecclesiastes 7:10
Ecclesiastes 10:8
Isaiah 1:16-20
Isaiah 55:6, 8
Jeremiah 15:19-21 — 1/4/08
Jeremiah 16;11,12 17
Jeremiah 17:5, 9
Ezekiel 3:11
Ezekiel 37:14

Joel 2:13
Amos 8:11
Matthew 6:19-21, 34
Matthew 7:1,2
Matthew 10:16, 22,23
Matthew 12:33-37
Mark 10:45
Mark 11:22
Luke 11:11-13
Luke 12:4,5
Luke 16:13-15
Luke 17:6
John 14:20,21
Romans 1:1,2
Romans 15:1-3
I Corinthians 1:4 — 9/13/07
I Corinthians 6:19,20
II Corinthians 10:3-5
Galatians 5:6, 22-26
Galatians 6:2
Ephesians 4:15 — 12/31/07
Ephesians 5:8-10
Philippians 2:4
Philippians 3:13,14 — 9/1/07
Philippians 4:4-9, 13
Colossians 3:14
Colossians 4:6
I Thessalonians 1:3
I Thessalonians 5:15
Hebrews 2:17,18
Hebrews 5:12
Hebrews 10:23 — 1/5/07
Hebrews10:35 — 10/1/06
Hebrews 12:1
Hebrews 13:15,16
James 1:12 — 1/3/07

James 1:26,27
James 3:13-16
James 4:7
James 5:14-16
I Peter 2:12, 15, 24
I Peter 4:7-11
I Peter 4:16 — 5/19/07
I Peter 4:19
I Peter 5:6 — 4/26/07
I John 1:8,9
I John 2:5,6, 15, 18
I John 3:18
I John 5:3-5, 14,15

PROTECTION

Psalm 3:3,4 — 10/7/07
Psalm 18:16
Psalm 28:6-9 — 7/1/07
Psalm 31:20
Psalm 34:7, 7-19
Psalm 73:21-28 — 7/23/07
Psalm 86:17 — 8/19/07
Psalm 91
Psalm 107:20
Psalm 121
Psalm 139:5
Proverbs 15:25 — 11/15/07
Proverbs 30:5, 8,9
Isaiah 43:1-7
Isaiah 49:25
Jeremiah 29:11 — 1/8/06
Lamentations 3:18

PROVISION

Hosea 6:6
Habakkuk 3:17-19
Zechariah 10:1,2
Malachi 3:10
Matthew 8:17
Matthew 16:19
Luke 8:15
II Corinthians 9:6-9, 11
Ephesians 6:10-20
Colossians 2:15
I John 4:4

TRUST

Psalm 33:20-22 — 1/27/06
Psalm 37:5-7 — 1/5/06
Psalm 40:1-3 — 9/3/07
Psalm 73:21-28
Psalm 92:15 — 6/7/08
Psalm 135:15-18
Psalm 143:8 — 1/30/06
Proverbs 3:5,6 — 9/06
Isaiah 2:22
Isaiah 26:3 — 1/4/06
Jeremiah 39:18

Coach Hep Indiana Cancer Challenge

According to the American Cancer Society, men have a one-in-two risk of developing some form of cancer throughout their lifetime and women a one-in-three risk. Indiana University football coach Terry Hoeppner was one of those individuals who was diagnosed with cancer — brain cancer. Coach Hep faced this situation with a positive "Don't Quit" attitude.

Since November 2006, a group of Bloomington professionals have dedicated their time, talents and resources to establish an event to promote the importance of cancer research and education and to keep Coach Terry Hoeppner's legacy alive.

Rick Schilling, a Bloomington physician, had treated many patients with cancer, but the disease struck him more personally when it killed his father-in-law, the daughter of a friend and then Coach Hep. So he decided to help organize an event to help fight it.

"This is a great opportunity to honor Coach Hep and his 'Don't Quit' attitude while supporting the fight against cancer right here in Indiana," Schilling said.

The Challenge is patterned after the Lance Armstrong Challenge Series, which is a cycle-run-walk event with participants obtaining pledges as individuals as well as teams.

Over the past two years the Coach Hep Indiana Cancer Challenge has taken shape into a successful community event that honors Coach Hep's determination and optimism while raising more than $50,000 for the IU Melvin and Bren Simon Cancer Center and the Olcott Center for Cancer Education.

In its third year, the Challenge seeks to reach out to a larger audience statewide and bring more participants to the event as well as raise record-breaking funds. The invaluable support of family, friends and the community will help the Challenge to meet, if not surpass, such goals.

We all have ties to cancer. That's why when you register for the Coach Hep Indiana Cancer Challenge, you receive a pair of red shoelaces. They're hard to miss, and a good way to remind friends and family members that we all benefit by supporting cancer treatment, research and education.

Have you been touched by cancer? Share your story and read personal accounts from people who have fought this disease by visiting:

www. CoachHepCancerChallenge.org.

Don't Quit. Join the Fight! **Saturday, May 1, 2010.**

About the Authors

Born and raised in Indianapolis, Jane Hoeppner now calls Bloomington, Indiana, home. She is the wife of late Indiana University football coach Terry Hoeppner. Jane is co-founder of the Coach Hep Indiana Cancer Challenge, a run- walk- bike event that raises money for cancer research. She is also active in Young Life, Hannah House/ Crisis Pregnancy Center, and Big Brother Big Sisters of South Central Indiana. Jane is a member of the Young Life Steering Committee and Sherwood Oaks Christian Church. Jane is also involved with the Capital Campaign for IU athletics. She is a former third grade teacher and curriculum coordinator.

Terry Hutchens has worked as a sportswriter for more than 30 years, including the past 19 at the Indianapolis Star. The past 12 years he has covered Indiana University football and basketball. In 2006 and again in 2008, Terry was honored as Indiana's Sportswriter of the Year by the National Sportswriters and Sportscasters Association. This is his third book. The first was *Let 'Er Rip* in 1996 and in 2007 he wrote *Hep Remembered: Memories of Terry Hoeppner* from those who knew him best. He's active at Holy Spirit at Geist Catholic Church where he sings in the contemporary choir and coaches CYO basketball. Terry resides with his wife of 23 years, Susan, and son Kevin in their home in Indianapolis. Another son, Bryan, is a freshman at Wabash College in Crawfordsville, Ind.

About the Photogapher

April Knox is a freelance photojournalist. She lives in Columbus, Ind. with her husband, Brian and their four children: Nick, Amanda, Adam and Joshua.

April's work can be seen monthly in *The Republic* and their many magazines: *She, Enjoy, Primetime, Business Connections,* and *Parent.*

April can be reached at:
April@intouchphotography.net

in Touch Photography.net

When you want someone to stay —
In touch with you …
In touch with the times …
You want —
In Touch Photography